The Road to Retirement

*Demographic and Economic
Changes in the 90s*

The Road to Retirement

Demographic and Economic Changes in the 90s

by Grant Schellenberg

Centre for International Statistics
Canadian Council on Social Development
Ottawa

The National Welfare Grants Program of Human Resources Development Canada is pleased to have provided financial support and consultation regarding the research, publication and dissemination of this project through the Senior Independence Research Program. The views expressed in this publication do not necessarily reflect those of Human Resources Development Canada.

CANADIAN CATALOGUING IN PUBLICATION DATA
Schellenberg, Grant, 1962-
The road to retirement: demographic and economic changes in the 90s

Includes bibliographical references.
ISBN 0-88810-427-8

1. Retirement—Canada.
2. Retirement—Economic aspects—Canada.
3. Retirement—Social aspects—Canada.
I. Canadian Council on Social Development.
II. Title.

HD7129.S37   1994   306.3'8'0971   C94-900771-4

Cover photograph:
Health Canada

Desktopping and cover art:
Accurate Design & Communication Inc.

Printed on:
Canadian-made recycled paper

Published by:
The Canadian Council on Social Development
55 Parkdale Avenue, P.O. Box 3505, Station C
Ottawa, Ontario K1Y 4G1
Tel: (613) 728-1865
Fax: (613) 728-9387

Ce livre est aussi disponible en français sous le titre :
La retraite : les changements démographiques et économiques des dernières années.

CONTENTS

Foreword

The Canadian Council on Social Development (CCSD) is pleased to publish this first volume from the Centre for International Statistics, the self-sustaining research arm of the CCSD. *The Road to Retirement* offers a detailed analysis of the different variables in the transition into retirement. It examines the ages at which people retire, the reasons why they retire, and how they finance their retirement. It also looks at differences across a range of demographic and socio-economic characteristics. The main source of information for the book is Statistics Canada's 1991 Survey on Ageing and Independence, although data from a variety of other sources has been incorporated.

Even though *The Road to Retirement* presents a substantial amount of statistical information, we hope that non-specialist readers will find it interesting and worthwhile. With the general aging of the population, more and more people are making the transition to retirement, but the conditions under which they are doing so are increasingly diverse. Pension benefits and financial incentives encourage some workers to leave the labour force, while layoffs and unemployment give others little choice in the matter. In the coming years, these trends will have repercussions on the well-being of all Canadians, on our ability to finance future social programs, and on our capacity to remain globally competitive.

In this initial volume from the Centre for International Statistics, I wish to draw a distinction between the publications of the Centre and those of the Council. Communications from the latter frequently provide more policy direction. The Centre, on the other hand, funds itself by undertaking contract research for governments as well as non-governmental organizations. Because most of this research becomes the property of its clients, which may include the CCSD, very little of the Centre's work is published under its own name. In this case, however, the research was the result of a contract with National Welfare Grants (NWG), now part of Human Resources Development Canada, which encouraged the Centre to publish the results. I would like to thank National Welfare Grants for its financial support.

Sharon Manson Singer
President, Canadian Council on Social Development

*For John and Lydia Schellenberg,
both of whom have followed
unusual roads to retirement.*

Acknowledgements

Many people have provided valuable assistance in the preparation of this book. I am grateful to Andrew Aitkens at One Voice: The Canadian Seniors Network for his generous contribution of time and expertise. And to Frank Fedyk at Health Canada who offered very useful comments on an earlier draft.

Most of the research at the Centre for International Statistics, including this book, is based on various Statistics Canada micro-data files. I want to thank Scott Murray and Kevin Bishop of the Household Surveys Division for their ongoing assistance, and Marc Levesque at the Labour Force Survey for responding to my numerous data requests over the telephone.

At the Canadian Council on Social Development and the Centre for International Statistics, I want to thank David Ross, Director, for his insights, support and patience, Clarence Lochhead and Richard Shillington for their many comments and suggestions, Angela Gibson-Kierstead for her help with the tables and her many trips to the library on my behalf, and Susan Scruton for her assistance with the charts. Roy Vontobel provided valuable editorial assistance, and Nancy Perkins supervised the production of the book. I also want to thank Diane Courtice for her encouragement and support.

Finally, this book would not have been possible without the financial contribution made by National Welfare Grants, now part of Human Resources Development Canada. Évariste Thériault deserves special acknowledgement for his support.

Grant Schellenberg
September 1994

List of Tables

APPENDIX

List of Charts

CHAPTER 1 About this Book

Retirement is like the automobile. In historic terms, both have been recent inventions. In their early development, both were luxuries enjoyed primarily by the wealthy, while in the last 40 years, both have become basic expectations for the majority of us. And like the automobile, the range of retirement models and options has proliferated in recent decades. There are many reasons for these developments.

The ways that people retire from their work and carry on with their lives have grown and adapted as the composition and dynamics of our society have evolved. Today our population, like those of many other Western nations, is made up of a growing number of older people. Between 1991 and 2011, the proportion of the Canadian population comprised of persons age 65 and over is forecast to grow from 12 to 15 per cent. And between the years 2011 and 2031, this proportion is projected to rise from 15 to 23 per cent, an absolute increase of 3.4 million people.[1] In the coming decades, more people than ever before will be making the transition into retirement.

Of these future retirees, a growing number will be women. No longer is the transition to retirement primarily a masculine concern. Moreover, differences in the circumstances of employment between women and men, including wage inequalities, occupational segregation and differing responsibilities for domestic labour, are reflected in this transition. Consequently, many of our conceptions of retirement, based on the experiences of men, are out of date and do not reflect the circumstances faced by many women.

As more and more women have entered the paid labour force, the employment profile of Canadian families has been altered. Dual-earner families, as a proportion of all husband-wife families, almost doubled, from 34 to 62 per cent, between 1967 and 1990.[2] The importance of considering two careers, rather than just one, in the retirement decision is a factor for a growing number of Canadians.

This is occurring at a time when the economic security of families has come under increasing pressure. Figures from a 1992 Angus Reid poll indicate that 50 per cent of middle-income Canadians (incomes between $30,000 and $60,000) believe they are worse off now than five years ago, and that "63 per cent expect their standard of living to remain the same or worsen in the next 10 years."[3] Individuals and families are now retiring and making retirement plans in a climate of uncertainty and insecurity.

Since the early 1980s, changing economic conditions have caused many firms to adopt strategies aimed at streamlining business operations. Production processes, corporate organization and labour relations have been restructured in response to increasing competition and new technology, and older workers have been profoundly affected by these changes. Companies have offered many workers financial incentives — early pensions or "golden handshakes" — to leave their jobs, using retirement itself as a mechanism for adjusting the makeup of the work force. But while some employees are enticed out of the labour force by financial inducements, others are simply pushed out by labour market conditions.

With unemployment rates persistently high since the early 1980s, many older workers have suffered job loss followed by long and often unsuccessful job searches. Given the many obstacles to reemployment, retirement is often a "better than nothing" alternative chosen by these workers. This situation is unlikely to improve in the coming years, as "jobless economic growth" is expected to continue.

Also transforming the retirement transition are the types of jobs being created. The former Economic Council of Canada estimated that almost half of all new employment generated throughout the 1980s was "non-standard" in form: self-employment, part-time employment, contract and fixed-term work. Such employment enables firms to tailor their work forces to market changes while avoiding the costs associated with maintaining permanent, full-time employees. To employees, it may offer new alternatives for partial or gradual retirement, allowing them to retain contact with the labour force while reducing their hours of work. On the other hand, because such non-standard work is often characterized by low wages, few benefits and little security, it may undermine the economic well-being of workers and make retirement more difficult.

Many political issues are intertwined with current changes in the modes of retirement. Most of the programs comprising Canada's old age security system, including the Canada/Quebec Pension Plans and Old Age Security, were designed on the assumption that entry into retirement and into "old age" were part of the same transition. This is no longer the case. Many people now retire from the labour force — often involuntarily — while still in their 50s. For those needing financial assistance, the old age security system is likely to be ineffective since they cannot begin to collect benefits at that age. This has raised concerns regarding the degree to which existing programs for retiring workers correspond to changing labour market conditions.

Government debt, at the federal, provincial and municipal levels, severely constrains public policy responses in all domains. Coupled with the aging population, this has fuelled worries about the long-term financial viability of social programs and the ability of younger workers to finance the pension and health care programs needed to sustain a growing number of elderly, non-employed Canadians. The merits of some policy responses, such as raising the age of public pension eligibility and increasing CPP/QPP contributions, are now being discussed in government as well as academic circles.

This book attempts to document the ongoing, and especially the most recent, transformation of retirement in our society. As a primary data source, we have used the Survey on Ageing and Independence (SAI), which was fielded in September 1991 by Statistics Canada in collaboration with several other federal government departments.[4] It contains information provided by 20,036 people, half of them between the ages of 45 and 64 and half aged 65 or older. These respondents are representative, on the whole, of the Canadian population aged 45 and over.[5] Besides the SAI, this study uses several other Statistics Canada surveys (the Survey of Consumer Finances, the Survey of Work Arrangement, and the Labour Force Survey) as well as published data from a wide variety of government and academic sources.

In the subsequent chapters, changes in the way people make the transition into retirement are examined along three dimensions.[6]

- **The Timing of Retirement**, and specifically, the trend towards retirement at younger ages, is examined in Chapter Three. It is argued that the timing of retirement has become destandardized. No longer do most people retire at or around age 65, as they did in the 1960s. Nowadays, retirement age varies widely, depending on individual circumstances, personal characteristics and desires.

- **The Process of Retirement**. Not only is the age of retirement changing, so too is the way people accomplish it. For some Canadians, it is preceded by a period of unemployment. For others, non-standard employment, such as a part-time job, allows them to gradually withdraw from the labour force. These and other labour market pathways to retirement are considered in Chapter Four. Chapter Five expands this analysis to the more subjective reasons for retirement, and confirms the importance of broader demographic and economic trends in altering the ways that people leave the work force and carry on their lives. At least one fact is incontrovertible: retirement in the 1990s is far different from what it was in earlier post-war decades.

- **The Financing of Retirement**, Chapter Six, addresses several issues. First, how are early retirees able to make ends meet? How do they survive financially when they have neither earnings from their labour nor income from public pensions? In fact, income from private sources, particularly employer-pensions, are the financial mainstay of these individuals. In spite of this, some public programs, particularly Disability Pensions administered through the Canada/Quebec Pension Plans (CPP/QPP), have come under increasing strain in recent years as the number of older workers receiving benefits has skyrocketed.

  Second, what are the sources of income among all retirees, of men and women in all socio-economic groups? A look at these shows that Canada's old age security system is two-sided: generally speaking, the most well-off retirees receive income from both public and semi-private sources, while the less fortunate are dependent upon public programs alone. Whether people are on one side or the other depends largely on their gender as well as their employment history.

  Finally, are the rich really getting richer and the poor poorer? In terms of retirement income, at least, the most well-off retirees continue to get the lion's share of that income while the poorest get very little. And there's been little change in this distribution over the past decade.

CHAPTER 2 Changing Times

Before considering the future of retirement, it is important to consider its past. Retirement in its current form is a relatively recent development. Through the nineteenth century and the early part of the twentieth, most Canadians worked in the labour force until they were no longer physically able to do so. In part, this was due to the fact that life expectancy was still relatively short, and only a small proportion of people lived beyond age 65.[1]

In a labour force transformed by the modern corporation, retirement would eventually become a key issue.

The nature of the economy also required many people to continue working on into old age. At the turn of the century, a far greater number of people than today were engaged in agricultural production, operating small and often economically precarious family farms. The distance between economic survival and ruin was often small, and withdrawal from economic activity was a luxury few could afford.[2] At the same time, however, ownership of a family farm or business did provide many Canadians with some security in old age. The transmission of property rights to younger family members in exchange for support in old age formed the basis for an intergenerational contract. This exchange allowed older persons "...to exploit ownership rights to obtain an income even as control was being passed on to the young."[3]

Retirement was also quite uncommon among persons employed as wage workers, due to the small size of most businesses and the close-knit nature of social relations. As the historian William Graebner notes, "Most businesses were not yet large enough to rationalize. The few dozen employees in a sawmill or shoe factory were not enough to share easily the financial burdens of forced retirement on a pension."[4] Close, personal relations between employers and employees and life in tight-knit communities also made dismissal of older workers unpleasant and infrequent.[5]

From the late nineteenth century on, however, the structure of the Canadian economy was dramatically altered. Increased agricultural productivity due to mechanization and advances in farming methods led to an exodus of people off the family farm. As shown in Chart 2.1, the proportion of the labour force engaged in agricultural production declined from about one-half in 1881 to about one-third in 1911. This precipitous decline continued throughout the following decades.

The modern corporation also emerged during this period. Business operations became increasingly concentrated and centralized in large, bureaucratically organized enterprises. In manufacturing, for example, the proportion of total employment in large firms (those with 500 or more workers) increased from 20 per cent to 30 per cent between 1922 and 1940. This represented an absolute increase of 138,000 workers. The proportion in small firms (those with fewer than 50 workers) declined from 28 to 24 per cent over the same period.[6] Similar changes occurred in other industries.

The exodus from the family farm and the emergence of the modern corporation transformed the labour force from one largely comprised of independent farmers and business owners to one comprised of wage and salaried employees. This had a tremendous impact on the nature of retirement.

It was within the modern corporation that formalized retirement policies first emerged. In Canada, the first formal pension plan was

Chart 2.1

Proportion of Labour Force Engaged in Agriculture, Canada, Various Years

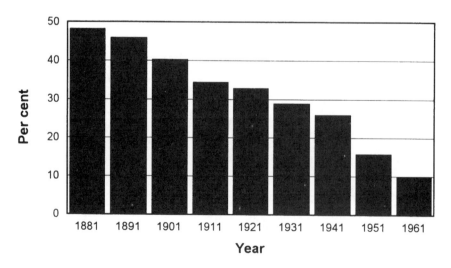

Source: Statistics Canada, *Historical Statistics of Canada*. Cat. CS11-516E, 1983.

The Road to Retirement

established by the federal government in 1870. Pensions appeared soon after in the railway industry, with both the Grand Trunk and the Canadian National Railways establishing plans in 1874.[7] In the first decades of the twentieth century, pension plans were established in most of the banks, railways and financial institutions. Similarly, in Britain, pensions and retirement policies were first introduced within branches of the civil service. In the United States they were first implemented by the railroad companies.[8]

Several factors motivated this development. In some industries, retirement policies were a response of employers to the growing strength of organized labour. The implementation of new programs for workers, including retirement pensions, were an attempt to quell worker discontent and foster company loyalty. This was especially the case where the geographic dispersion of workers, as in the railway industry, made traditional methods of supervision and control impractical.[9] Because pensions were designated as gifts from the employer rather than as legal entitlements for workers, they could be revoked at any time and used as the proverbial dangling carrot (or big stick) to persuade labour to be cooperative.

Support for retirement was also fuelled by the adoption of new forms of business organization and methods of production. During the 1920s and 1930s, new methods of production were instituted in accordance with the principles of "scientific management." Production processes were broken down into their smallest component steps, so they could be completed by workers with minimal skills. As the steps involved in work tasks were reduced, the speed of production was increased. This rationalization of production extended to the labour force itself. Workers were selected for their efficiency and speed, and, on that basis, older workers were increasingly viewed as unsuitable for employment.[10]

This view was reinforced by the introduction of new technologies. Following the installation of expensive new machinery, employers were keen to boost productivity in order to recoup their capital investments. In many industries, tremendous pressure was placed on workers to sustain high levels of output throughout the day — too high, managers reasoned, for older workers to sustain.[11]

With the reorganization of business operations and production methods, the older worker was increasingly viewed as an obstacle to productivity. This sentiment was reflected in a study entitled *Industrial Retirement Plans in Canada*, published by the Industrial

Relations Section at Queen's University in 1938.[12] The study recognized that economic necessity, rather than humanitarian motives alone, had fuelled the adoption of retirement policies in most firms.[13] The issue of productivity lay at the heart of this development:

> The seriousness of the problem of employee obsolescence has forced itself more and more on the attention of management. The quickened pace of modern industry has made the employment of aged workers unprofitable, while the growing intensity of competition has necessitated closer attention to economies in personnel administration. Men, like machines, inevitably reach a stage of lessening efficiency, and it is expedient to replace them with new and better material.[14]

As economic benefits of retirement policies, the report also cited the improvement of morale, the facilitation of promotions, the attraction of better workers, the creation of favourable public opinion, the reduction of labour turnover and the reduction of strike activity.

In a similar vein, Adam Shortt, the first civil service commissioner, made an ardent case for mandatory retirement within the federal government in 1922. In his words, this would serve the public interest

> ...as it relieves the government of the embarrassment and extravagance of retaining the services of officers who have outlived their usefulness, creates a proper flow of promotions, renders the service more mobile, deters efficient workers from leaving the public service for private employment...[and] in general tends to promote efficiency in every way.[15]

Overall, managers viewed retirement as a mechanism for work force adjustment, enabling them to replace older workers with younger, more efficient and less expensive ones. Support for retirement was reinforced by the high levels of unemployment during the Depression of the 1930s. Employers, unions and governments advocated the retirement of older workers as a way to open up job opportunities for the young.

In many cases, organized labour also endorsed the establishment of retirement pensions. Traditionally, unions supported indigent members through relief funds. However, these funds faced considerable pressures during economic downturns and were far from sufficient to sustain large numbers of old or disabled workers. Pensions provided a viable alternative, allowing unions to restructure their relief functions in a more systematic fashion. Pensions also helped organized labour to recruit and retain new members, and to open up jobs for younger workers while ensuring the well-being of older ones.

There was also strong union support for a public pension system in Canada. The Trades and Labor Congress of Canada adopted a recommendation supporting such a system at its annual convention in 1905, and over the following years continued to lobby the government to take steps in this direction.[16] Evidence suggests the situation was similar in Britain and the United States, with organized labour in both countries pressing for public pension programs.[17] However, some writers have suggested that certain unions opposed pension initiatives, since they regarded them as a ploy to co-opt workers and foster their allegiance to the corporation and the state.[18]

The meaning of retirement has been largely shaped by the post-war welfare state.

In spite of widespread support from employers, labour and government, retirement did not emerge prior to the Second World War. This was primarily because there was no "institutionalized system of income provision" for those who would be excluded from the labour market if retirement were widely implemented.[19] Although a number of income sources for the older worker did exist, they were very limited.

At the turn of the century, most municipalities and charitable organizations provided some form of support for the needy. However, the financial resources of these organizations were limited and inadequate for anything except the provision of assistance in emergency situations. Similarly, private and public institutions provided some assistance to older people, but on an extremely small scale.[20]

There are few data on the personal savings of Canadians prior to the Second World War. However, the underdevelopment of institutionalized mechanisms for long-term savings, such as annuities, investment trusts and mutual funds, suggests that few Canadians had the resources to save significant amounts for their old age.[21] In 1931, there were only 15,370 annuity contracts (including public and private contracts) registered in Canada. In 1941, there were 105,744 — at a time when there were 768,000 people aged 65 and older.

Similarly, private pensions remained limited prior to the Second World War despite their initial emergence 50 to 75 years earlier. The Dominion Bureau of Statistics reported that of the pension plans included in its survey in 1947, more than two-thirds had been implemented after 1939. In terms of the proportion of the labour force with pension coverage, one writer suggests 10 to 15 per cent is a "reasonable guess." [22]

Public pensions were also very restricted. Canada's first public pension was established with the passage of the Old Age Pension Act in 1927. The Old Age Pension provided a means-tested benefit to persons over age 70, and was designed to supplement the incomes of the poor, not replace employment earnings for older workers leaving the labour force.[23] In 1928, during the program's first full year of operation, fewer than 3,000 people received benefits. This climbed to 58,000 by 1931, but, nonetheless, fewer than one in five people aged 70 or over received benefits. Coverage broadened somewhat in the following decades, but even in its last year of operation (1951), fewer than half of Canadians aged 70 and over received benefits through the program (see Table 2.1).

Overall, considerable support for the principle of retirement had been generated before the Second World War. But, the financial means to facilitate the adoption of this principle remained undeveloped. Most men stayed in the labour force well into their 60s, and most women were excluded from paid employment altogether. Table 2.2 shows the labour force participation rates of men and women aged 65 and over between 1921 and 1951. (Participation rates show the number of people in the labour force, both employed and unemployed, as a proportion of the total population.) Prior to 1941, the majority of men aged 65 and over remained in the labour force, although their participation declined somewhat during this period, reflecting job loss through the Depression and the moderate extension of private pensions and the Old Age Pension program. By today's standard, however, a very high proportion of older men remained in the labour force.

Table 2.1

Recipients of Old Age Pensions, Canada 1928 - 1951

	Number of Old Age Pension Recipients	Recipients as a Proportion of Population Aged 70 or Over
1928	2,700	-
1931	57,900	17%
1935	101,100	-
1941	185,900	40%
1945	187,500	-
1951	302,200	46%

The Old Age Pension was implemented in 1927 and replaced by the Old Age Security program in 1952.

Source: Statistics Canada, *Historical Statistics of Canada*. Cat CS11-516E, Series C287-299, 1983.

The state of retirement changed in the post-war period. Federal and provincial governments undertook unprecedented responsibility for the redistribution of national income, with support for seniors a major consideration. The guiding purpose underlying government initiatives changed from the pre-war period. "No longer was it sufficient to provide a safety net for those who fell out of the market; instead, the goal became that of providing a retirement wage sufficient to replace the market wage."[24]

Several programs were implemented. In 1952, the Old Age Security program was initiated, providing universal benefits for Canadians aged 65 and over. By 1958, 850,000 Canadians were beneficiaries and by 1966 this figure topped one million.[25] In 1966, the Canada/Quebec Pension Plans (CPP/QPP) were introduced, followed by the Guaranteed Income Supplement (GIS) in 1967. By 1975, almost 500,000 Canadians were receiving CPP/QPP benefits and over 1 million were receiving the GIS.[26]

Private pensions also became more widespread. In the late 1940s and early 1950s, organized labour in the automobile industry made pensions a key contract demand. Unions in other industries soon followed suit.[27]

This access to public, and to a lesser extent, private pensions provided an increasing number of older workers with the financial means to withdraw from the labour force. With access to such support, the rise in the number of people retiring was dramatic. The labour force participation rate of men aged 65 and over fell from 48 per cent in 1947 to 25 per cent in 1968, and continued this decline to 10 per cent in 1993.[28]

Overall, the development of the post-war welfare state has been central in the widespread implementation of retirement. By the late 1960s, retirement at (or near) age 65 became prevalent in most Western nations.[29] The central role of the welfare state in this has had a number of implications.

Table 2.2

Labour Force Participation Rates of Men and Women Aged 65 and Over, Canada, 1921 - 1951

	Men	Women
1921	59.6	6.6
1931	56.5	6.2
1941	47.9	5.8
1951	39.5	4.5

Source: Frank Denton, *The Growth of Manpower in Canada*. Dominion Bureau of Statistics, Cat. CS99-556/ 1969, 1970, Table 7.

First, our understanding of the course of people's lives has been shaped around state institutions. As Anne-Marie Guillemard notes, the life course in Western industrial societies has been divided into three stages: *youth*, characterized by participation in the education system; *adulthood*, characterized by participation in work; and *old age*, characterized by retirement and participation in the old age security system.[30] In this division, retirement and old age have been "almost synonymous." Exit from the labour market and entry into "old age" have been two sides of the same transition. At the same time, eligibility for government programs, such as the Canada/Quebec Pension Plans and Old Age Security, has signified the boundary between adulthood and old age.

Second, the meaning of retirement in the post-war period has been shaped by the welfare state. If one is retired, one is also likely to be "old" (formally defined as age 65 or older), receiving a public pension, and out of the paid labour force. However, this combination of characteristics of retirement is becoming undone. Many people now retire in their 50s and cannot be considered "old" in any sense of the term. They are also excluded from the old age security system. As Guillemard argues, this is undermining the threefold model of the life course as it has been defined in the post-war period and is dissolving conventional views of "old age as retirement."[31]

Defining Retirement Today

Retirement has never been a static phenomenon, but has been changing for more than a hundred years. And this transformation continues. These days, when someone tells you he or she is retiring, you cannot be entirely certain what that means. It has been said that retirement "... can refer to an event, a process, a role or status, or a phase of life,"[32] but that is just another way of saying the term has become ambiguous. This can be a problem for a researcher trying to put people in different conceptual pigeonholes. Different definitions of retirement may influence estimates of how many people are retired, what their demographic and socio-economic characteristics are, and so on. Consider the following.

Subjective definitions

Retirement may be defined in subjective terms; that is to say, people are retired when they identify themselves as such, regardless of their labour force activities or sources of income. One pitfall of this approach is that people who may be viewed as retired in more "objective" terms may not perceive themselves as such. For example, many older women who have left the paid labour force do not consider themselves to be retired.[33] Their self-definition appears to be based on their relationship to their families rather than to the labour force. Many would call themselves "housewives" or "homemakers" rather than "retirees," in spite of their withdrawal from the paid labour force after years of employment.

Labour force definitions

Retirement may also be defined in terms of labour force activity. For example, one may simply define as "retired" all persons over a specific age (such as age 55 or 60) who have previously been employed, but have permanently left the labour force. One implication of this approach is that it includes housewives or other people who have left paid employment, but who do not perceive themselves to be retired. On the other hand, persons who consider themselves retired but who work on a part-time or self-employed basis would not be included.

Partial labour market withdrawal also may be used to define retirement. For example, once a person's hours of work fall below a fraction of their previous hours (for example, one-half), they may be considered retired.[34]

Income-based definitions

Many writers define retirement on the basis of income sources.[35] For example, all persons receiving income from a public pension (such as the Canada/Quebec Pension Plans) or an employer-pension may be counted as retired. Alternatively, all persons who no longer have income from wages and salaries may be counted. People who are not covered by employer-pensions or who withdraw from paid labour before they are eligible for a public pension are not counted as retired using these definitions.

Retirement is a slippery concept. The problems associated with each definitional approach are likely to increase in the coming years because of the growing diversity in how and when people retire. Some researchers have argued that dichotomous retired/non-retired categories fail to capture this diversity, and that more sophisticated definitions are needed.[36]

The Survey on Ageing and Independence definition

In undertaking statistical research, the definition of retirement used is often dictated by the nature of the data. This is the case in this study. The Survey on Ageing and Independence (SAI) is the primary data set on which this book is based. The survey is structured around both a subjective and a labour force definition of retirement. "Retirees" are survey respondents aged 45 years of age and over who identify themselves as retired, and who have permanently stopped working full-time for pay or profit or looking for full-time employment. People who have never had a paying job are not counted as retired. Respondents who identify themselves as retired, and who are working part-time or looking for part-time work, are counted as retired.

Using this definition, there are 1.1 million retired men and 792,000 retired women aged 45 and over in Canada. Table 2.3 shows retirees as a proportion of the population. Twenty-two per cent of men and 15 per cent of women aged 55 to 64 are retired. Among men, about seven in ten of those aged 65 to 74 and eight in ten of those aged 75 and over are retired. Among women aged 65 and over, slightly less than four in ten are retired.

But what are the characteristics of these retirees? At what age did they retire? Why did they retire? How do they make ends meet financially? Is the retirement experience faced by people in their 50s different from that previously faced by people in their 70s or 80s? It is to these and other questions we now turn.

Table 2.3

Proportion of the Population that is Retired by Age Group and Sex, Canada, 1991 (per cent)

	All	Men	Women
55 to 64	19	22	15
65 to 74	51	67	37
75 & over	53	79	36

Source: Prepared by the Centre for International Statistics using Survey on Ageing and Independence microdata, 1991.

CHAPTER 3 The Timing of Retirement

Government legislation and institutions have a remarkable capacity for defining the stages of our lives. Since the mid-1960s, age 65 has been formally recognized in Canada as the start of old age, with eligibility for the Canada/Quebec Pension Plans (CPP/QPP), Old Age Security (OAS), the Guaranteed Income Supplement (GIS), and other programs set at this age. In other Western nations, this has also been the case. Labour market exit and eligibility for public pensions at or around age 65 has been "surprisingly uniform."[1] Private pensions have followed suit. This age has been a legal and programmatic reference point, as well as a behavioural and labour force reference point.[2]

Since the mid-1960s, age 65 has been formally recognized in Canada as the start of old age.

In this context, age 65 has provided a clear-cut and predictable terminus to labour force participation. Through the 1950s and 1960s, the male pattern was one of full-time uninterrupted employment followed by a clearly defined and foreseeable exit from work.[3] Some workers, such as miners or loggers, might have retired from their physically demanding occupations before age 65, but overall the timing of retirement was relatively standardized. Individual circumstances and characteristics may have shaped the quality of retirement, but variation in the timing of retirement was limited.

Since the 1960s, however, this uniformity has been increasingly challenged. There has been a marked trend towards retirement at younger ages, and while many people still retire at age 65, many others now do so before well before this age (see Chart 3.1).

Likewise, there is great variation in retirement expectations; of those persons still in the labour force today, only a small proportion expect to retire at age 65. So while this age may remain an important reference point for public programs, such as the CPP/QPP, and for legal issues such as mandatory retirement, it is decreasingly a reference point for the labour market decisions of Canadians. With this tremendous variation, then, the timing of retirement has become destandardized. Individuals retire at very different ages and eligibility for a public pension is no longer the key factor around which retirement is organized.[4] Instead, individual circumstances and characteristics play an increasingly important role.

The Trend Towards Early Retirement

The movement of workers out of the labour force at younger and younger ages has been one of the most striking economic trends since the Second World War. The extent of this can be measured using labour force participation rates. In its estimates for 16 countries, the Organisation for Economic Cooperation and Development (OECD) reports that labour force participation rates of persons aged 55 and over declined by an average of almost 13 percentage points between 1966 and 1990. This trend is shown for selected countries in Table 3.1. In Canada, the rate declined by 10 percentage points, from 36.4 to 26.5 per cent over this period. In the United States the pattern is similar, while in the United Kingdom and Germany, participation rates declined by almost 20 percentage points. In Sweden, there remains a higher rate of labour force participation among older workers, although there, too, this rate has been in decline.

However, these figures conceal important differences across sex and age groups. Almost all of the decline in participation rates is accounted for by the exit of older men from the labour force. As shown in Table 3.2, the participation rate for men aged 55 and

Chart 3.1

Retired Canadians: Age at Retirement 1991

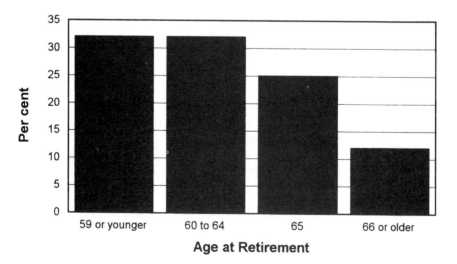

Source: Prepared by the Centre for International Statistics, using *Survey on Ageing and Independence* microdata, 1991.

The Road to Retirement

Table 3.1

Labour Force Participation Rates for Persons Aged 55 and Over, Selected Nations, 1966 - 1990

	Canada	United States	United Kingdom	Germany	Sweden
1966	36.4	37.7	53.8	40.5	47.4
1975	32.9	33.5	48.0	23.4	42.0
1980	31.3	31.7	42.0	22.1	40.1
1985	28.9	29.3	36.5	20.7	39.0
1990	26.5	29.1	36.5	na	39.7

Source: OECD, *Employment Outlook*, *July 1992*. Paris: OECD, 1992, Table 5.1.

over declined by almost 20 percentage points between 1966 and 1990, while the rate for women remained stable.

The relatively stable rate among women reflects the interplay of two forces. On the one hand, the rate has been pushed upwards by the widespread entry of women into the paid labour force through the post-war period. On the other hand, it has been pushed downwards by the general tendency towards early retirement.[5] Because the number of men entering the labour force has not increased, the downward pressure exerted by early retirement for them has not been offset as it has been for women.

Noticeable differences are also evident across age groups. The participation rate of men aged 65 and over declined steadily through the post-war period, dropping from 47.5 per cent in 1946 to 23.5 per cent in 1969. By 1993, only 10 per cent were labour force participants (see Appendix 3.1).

Among men aged 60 to 64, the rate was still quite high in 1961, at approximately 79 per cent.[6] It declined to 74.1 per cent by 1971, and to 68.3 per cent by 1981. But it was through the 1980s that the most precipitous decline occurred, with the rate dropping 15 percentage points — from 68.3 to 53.6 — in 10 years. Clearly, the withdrawal of older men was greatly accelerated during this period. The consequences of economic restructuring, including

Table 3.2

Labour Force Participation Rates for Men and Women Aged 55 and Over, Canada 1966 - 1990

	Men	Women
1966	56.7	18.0
1975	50.5	17.6
1980	46.5	18.3
1985	42.1	17.9
1990	37.4	17.4

Source: Calculations by author using Statistics Canada, *Historical Labour Force Statistics*, Cat. 71-201, 1992.

layoffs and incentives for early retirement, as well as changes to CPP/QPP legislation allowing partial benefits at age 60, fuelled this increase.

Men aged 55 to 59 also began to leave the labour force at a greater rate during this period. Before 1981, their participation rate remained above 82 per cent. But over the following decade it dropped from 83.9 to 77.8 per cent. This drop has continued into the 1990s.

Labour market exit now appears to be occurring among even younger men. The first signs of declining participation among men aged 45 to 54 appeared during the early 1990s. The participation rate of this age group remained around 91 to 92 per cent through the 1970s and 1980s, but dropped below 91 per cent for the first time in 1991, and continued to drop in the following two years to 89.7 per cent in 1993. This decline is slight, to be sure, but it may well be the precursor of a more significant shift of men aged 45 to 54 out of the labour force.

Data from the Survey on Ageing and Independence confirm the trend towards earlier retirement. Table 3.4 shows that larger proportions of men and women in younger age groups retired before age 60 and before age 65. This indicates that early retirement is more prevalent now than 20 years ago. However, the incidence of death among older age groups may influence this pattern to some extent. Early retirees in older age groups, particularly those who retired for health reasons, are more likely to have died than early retirees in younger

Table 3.3

Labour Force Participation Rates by Age Group and Sex , Canada 1961 - 1991

| | Men | | Women | |
	Age 55-59	Age 60-64	Age 55-59	Age 60-64
1961*	81.9		24.4	
1971	84.9	74.1	38.7	29.1
1976	82.4	69.0	39.2	27.3
1981	83.9	68.3	41.7	28.1
1986	80.7	59.3	44.3	27.2
1991	77.8	53.6	49.7	27.9

*Includes persons aged 55 to 64

Source: Dominion Bureau of Statistics, 1961 Census *Labour Force: Employment Status by Sex* , Cat. 94-533, December 1964. Statistics Canada, *The Nation: Labour Force Activity* , Cat. 93-324, March 1993.

The Road to Retirement

age groups, thereby distorting comparisons. Because we are dealing only with survivors, the effect of this cannot be estimated.

As already stated, people who have yet to retire express a wide range of retirement intentions.[7] Two-thirds of them expect to retire and are able to state the age at which they plan to do so. One-quarter expect to retire, but are uncertain of when this will occur. And one in ten indicate they will not retire.

The popularity of early retirement is evident among those stating their expected retirement age: 28 per cent plan to retire before age 60, and 62 per cent plan on doing so before age 65. The Survey on Ageing and Independence does not provide any information on how many of these retirement expectations will actually be fulfilled, nor on how many retirees fulfilled their expectations in the past. Other research indicates that, at most, two-thirds of workers actually retire at the age which they had previously planned, even when they were within a few years of retirement to begin with.[8] This suggests the retirement plans of many people are off-target.

It is also the case that retirement intentions fluctuate over time, with people planning and replanning their retirement with greater certainty as they reach their late 50s and early 60s.[9] For some, good health and economic security allow them to reach their objectives. Others are forced into retirement earlier or later than expected by unforeseen events, such as health problems or job loss.

Given these factors, it is likely that many of these retirement expectations will not be fulfilled. However, some will be. And whether fulfilled or not, these expectations vary consistently across income, education and other factors, suggesting that there are

Table 3.4

Retired Canadians: Early Retirement by Age Group and Sex, Canada, 1991

	% Within Age Group Retired Before Age 60		% Within Age Group Retired Before Age 65	
	Men	Women	Men	Women
60 to 64	60	60	-	-
65 to 69	20	29	66	72
70 to 74	16	27	48	60
75 to 79	9	17	36	44
80 or over	3	14	23	43

Source: Prepared by the Centre for International Statistics using Survey on Ageing and Independence microdata, 1991.

significant differences in the way people experience (or anticipate) retirement. It is also noteworthy that many of the factors associated with expectations of retirement at different ages are very similar to the factors associated with *actual* retirement at these ages. For these reasons, the factors associated with actual *and* expected retirement at different ages are included in the chapter.

Age of Retirement and Labour Market Characteristics

The labour market experiences of men and women differ along many dimensions, including occupation, unionization, wages, hours worked and so on. So, perhaps it is not surprising that the age of retirement, too, differs between the sexes. As shown in Chart 3.2, women tend to retire earlier than men, with 38 per cent of female retirees leaving the labour force before age 60 compared to 27 per cent of men.[10]

Among those still in the labour force, the proportion of women who expect to retire before age 60 (30 per cent) is only slightly larger than the proportion of men (26 per cent). Beyond this, the

Chart 3.2

**Retired Men and Women: Age at Retirement
Canada, 1991**

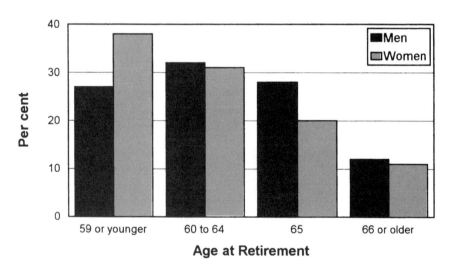

Source: Prepared by the Centre for International Statistics, using *Survey on Ageing and Independence* microdata, 1991.

retirement expectations of men and women are very similar, varying by only two to three percentage points. Very few Canadians of either sex expect to retire after age 65.

Occupation

A number of studies indicate that "professional and managerial workers are far more likely to remain employed at older ages than labourers, operatives and craftsworkers." [11] Broadly speaking, this has been interpreted in terms of a blue-collar/white-collar (or manual/non-manual) divide, with workers from the latter occupations more likely to defer retirement.[12] This is often explained in terms of the physical demands of blue-collar occupations and the declining ability of workers to remain in them at older ages. Explanations based on worker productivity and job satisfaction have also been offered, with persons in white-collar positions viewed as more likely to defer retirement because they derive greater satisfaction from their work and are better able to sustain their productivity until older ages.

Analysis of the Survey on Ageing and Independence indicates that retired men in professional, managerial and technical occupations

Chart 3.3

Employed Men and Women: Expected Age of Retirement Canada, 1991

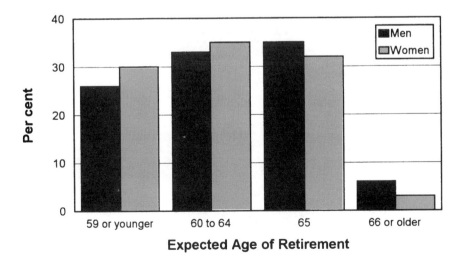

Source: Prepared by the Centre for International Statistics, using *Survey on Ageing and Independence* microdata. 1991.

have a broader "window of retirement" than those in semi-skilled and unskilled occupations. That is, men in the former categories are more likely to defer retirement past age 65 *and* they are more likely to retire before age 60. They exhibit a fairly wide range of retirement ages. Conversely, men in semi-skilled and unskilled occupations retire within a narrower "window" — between the ages of 60 and 65 (see Appendix 3.2).

There may be several reasons for this. Men in professional and managerial jobs tend to earn relatively high wages and are more likely than men in other occupations to receive financial incentives to retire early. These income sources provide the resources for retirement at younger ages. On the other hand, conventional explanations regarding job satisfaction, worker productivity and health factors probably account for why some men in these jobs choose to defer retirement to an older age. Men from professional and managerial occupations are also among the most likely to

Chart 3.4

Retired and Employed Men: Per Cent Retiring/ Expecting to Retire Before Age 60, by Occupation Canada, 1991

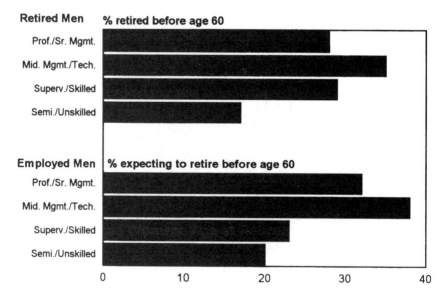

Source: Prepared by the Centre for International Statistics, using *Survey on Ageing and Independence* microdata, 1991.

The Road to Retirement

return to paid employment following their initial retirement and to find alternative forms of employment, as consultants, for example. These alternative work arrangements are no doubt an important factor in their ability to defer retirement until they are older.

Compared to men, women show a greater tendency towards early retirement in all occupations. Again, early retirement is most prevalent among women from professional and managerial positions, although relatively large proportions of women from other occupations also retire early. There are few differences in the prevalence of late retirement among women in the other occupational categories.

In terms of expectations regarding retirement, men and women in white-collar positions, again, are most likely to expect to retire before age 60, while those in semi-skilled and unskilled occupations are least likely to expect that. As noted earlier, very few employed respondents, regardless of occupation, expect to retire after age 65.

Chart 3.5

Retired and Employed Women: Per Cent Retiring/ Expecting to Retire Before Age 60, by Occupation Canada, 1991

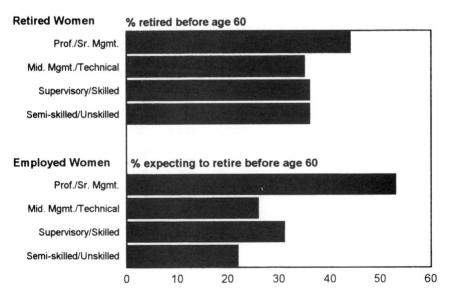

Source: Prepared by the Centre for International Statistics, using *Survey on Ageing and Independence* microdata. 1991.

Education

Given the relation of education to occupation, it is not surprising to find that the timing of retirement also varies across levels of education. Individuals who have had more education are more likely to retire early than those who have not. To be more specific, men and women who have not completed high school are much less likely to retire, or expect to retire, before age 60 than those who have completed high school or a post-secondary program.

As far as late retirement is concerned, however, level of education does not appear to be a significant factor. The proportions of men and women retiring or expecting to retire at age 66 or older generally vary by less than 2 to 3 percentage points.

Employer-pension plans

There is a consensus within the literature that men with employer-pension coverage are more likely to retire early than those without such coverage.[13] This is most commonly interpreted as "pension pull,"

Chart 3.6

Men: Actual and Expected Ages of Retirement by Employer-Pension Coverage, Canada 1991

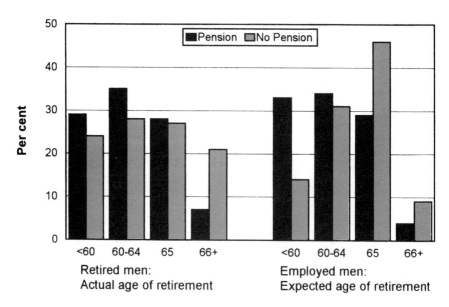

Source: Prepared by the Centre for International Statistics, using *Survey on Ageing and Independence* microdata, 1991.

that is, pension income provides a financial incentive to leave the labour force. This relationship is confirmed by the Survey on Ageing and Independence (see Charts 3.6 and 3.7). But while it holds for men, the data suggest that pension coverage is not a significant predictor of retirement for women.[14] In fact, women with such coverage appear to be *less* likely to retire before age 60 than women without. This relationship is not evident when the retirement expectations of women still in the labour force are considered.

Class of worker

The timing of retirement is also associated with the form of labour force participation. In general, self-employed men and women are more likely to defer retirement past age 65 than those who are wage and salaried employees.[15] There are two possible explanations for this. First, because self-employed individuals have more control over their work patterns than do paid employees, they may be better able to gradually reduce their hours of work and ease into retirement in a step-by-step fashion. Alternatively, because they have lower average

Chart 3.7

Women: Actual and Expected Ages of Retirement by Employer-Pension Coverage, Canada 1991

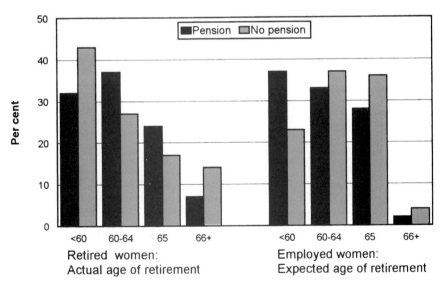

Source: Prepared by the Centre for International Statistics, using *Survey on Ageing and Independence* microdata, 1991.

earnings than paid workers, inadequate savings and economic insecurity may be the cause of their greater propensity to defer retirement.

Labour market status, job tenure and weeks worked [16]

Labour market status, job tenure and number of weeks worked are all associated with expectations of retirement at earlier ages (see Chart 3.8). Persons employed on a full-time basis, who have been in the same job for many years, and who work on a full-year basis are more likely to expect to retire early than those working part-time, part-year and for shorter periods.

If these variables are taken as measures of job security, the data demonstrate that job security is positively associated with expectations of earlier retirement. This is the case if early retirement is defined as withdrawal from paid labour either before age 60 or before age 65, and is generally the case for both men and women. At the other end of the spectrum, there is some evidence

Chart 3.8

Per Cent of Canadians Expecting to Retire Before Age 60, by Selected Characteristics, 1991

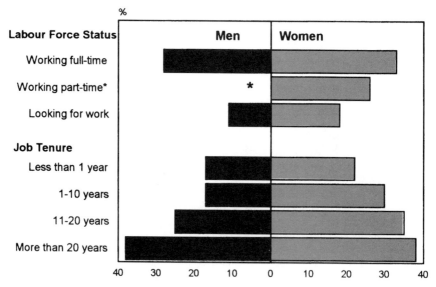

*Sample size too small to provide estimate.

Source: Prepared by the Centre for International Statistics, using *Survey on Ageing and Independence* microdata, 1991.

to suggest that less job security is associated with greater expectations of late retirement, although overall relatively few men and women expect to defer retirement past age 65.

Personal income

Finally, labour market resources are perhaps best measured using personal income. In the Survey on Ageing and Independence, data are available only on respondents' *current income*, as opposed to their income prior to retirement. One might assume that higher current incomes reflect higher incomes before retirement, but the validity of this cannot be tested using the Survey.

Among retired Canadians, current income and retirement timing appear to be associated. Among men, a larger proportion of individuals with current personal incomes of $40,000 or more retired before age 60 than did those with lower incomes. Similarly, men with higher incomes are less likely to have retired at age 65 or older.

One exception to this is a relatively large proportion of men with current incomes of less than $10,000 who retired before age 60 (31 per cent). One likely explanation is that illness, disability, job loss or other factors pushed these workers out of the labour force and into "retirement" at early ages. Indeed, a disproportionate number of these early retirees with low incomes say they retired because of health problems. As will be documented in Chapters Four and Five, there are many "pathways" into retirement, and some involve involuntary labour force exit at an early age and economic insecurity in old age.

Among women, the association between personal income and age of retirement is unclear. Again, a large proportion of women with current personal incomes of less than $10,000 retired before age 60 (50 per cent). In addition to the effects of early retirement due to health problems, job loss or family responsibilities, this may also be attributable to the prevalence of part-time and sporadic employment among women in the labour force. This results in lower retirement income because of exclusion from employer-pension plans, lower contributions to the Canada/Quebec Pension Plans, and lower personal savings and investments.

Among working Canadians expecting to retire, there is a clear and consistent association between income and the expected age of retirement. Men and women with higher personal incomes are more likely to anticipate an early retirement than those with lower incomes. For example, 33 per cent of men with incomes of $60,000 or more expect to retire before age 60 compared to 14 per cent of those with incomes of $10,000 to $19,999. On the other hand, correlations between personal income and expectations of late retirement (after age 65) are almost non-existent. The vast majority of Canadians, regardless of income, expect to retire at age 65 or younger.

Overall, actual and expected early retirement (before age 60) is most prevalent among individuals in managerial and professional occupations, among individuals with higher levels of education, and, especially for men, among individuals with larger personal incomes. Moreover, earlier retirement is positively associated with coverage under an employer-pension plan, longer job tenure and full-time employment. While individuals who do not have these characteristics may also retire early, they are less likely to do so.

Chart 3.9

Retired Men and Women: Per Cent Retiring Before Age 60 by Sex and Personal Income, Canada 1991

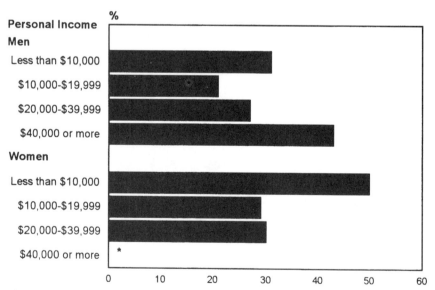

*Sample size too small to provide estimate.

Source: Prepared by the Centre for International Statistics, using *Survey on Ageing and Independence* microdata, 1991.

The Road to Retirement

Chart 3.10

Per Cent of Canadians Expecting to Retire Before Age 60 by Sex and Personal Income, 1991

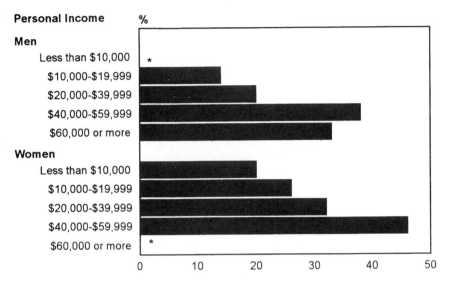

*Sample sizes too small to provide estimates.

Source: Prepared by the Centre for International Statistics, using *Survey on Ageing and Independence* microdata, 1991.

Age of Retirement and Family Characteristics

People do not exist solely as workers in the labour force, but also as members of families. It is important to consider the characteristics of these families in the retirement transition. As noted in Chapter One, the proportion of husband-wife families with two earners almost doubled between 1967 and 1990, making it increasingly necessary to consider two careers (and incomes), rather than just one, in the retirement decision.[17] Other factors also are changing. Compared to the 1960s, people are now getting married and having children at later ages.[18] This, coupled with the trend towards early retirement, may mean that retirement plans must increasingly take into account the presence of children in the home.

Marital status

The importance of family context is evident in the influence of marital status on the retirement decision. Married (or common-law) women are more likely to retire earlier (or expect to retire earlier) than non-married women. As shown in Chart 3.11, while half of married women retire before age 60, only 28 per cent of non-married women do so. This difference carries over into the categories of later retirement, with married women much less likely to defer retirement past age 65 than their non-married counterparts.

This pattern is also evident among women still in the labour force (see Chart 3.12). The proportion of married women expecting to retire before age 60 is twice that of non-married women (35 and 17 per cent respectively). These differences are much less evident among men.

One interpretation of these results is that married women undertake "joint retirement" at the same time as their spouse, and retire earlier in order to do so.[19] Because women tend to be slightly younger than their husbands, this would account for the greater prevalence of early retirement among married women.

An alternative interpretation is that non-married women lack the resources to withdraw from the labour force before age 60 while

Chart 3.11

Retired Men and Women: Age at Retirement by Sex and Marital Status, Canada 1991

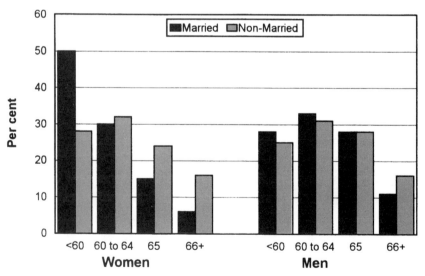

Source: Prepared by the Centre for International Statistics, using *Survey on Ageing and Independence* microdata, 1991.

Chart 3.12

Expected Age of Retirement by Sex and Marital Status Canada 1991

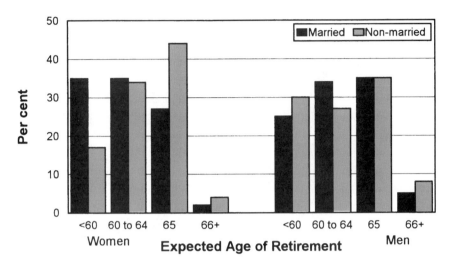

Source: Prepared by the Centre for International Statistics, using *Survey on Ageing and Independence* microdata, 1991.

married women do not. As will be shown in Chapter Five, household income is a key determinant in one's ability to make adequate financial preparations for retirement. Non-married women, who typically live in households with lower average incomes than married women, may be less able to prepare for retirement.

Household income

The importance of family security in the retirement decision is underscored when household income is considered. Overall, people in households with higher incomes are more likely to retire before age 60, or to expect to retire before age 60, than individuals in households with lower incomes. This is shown in Chart 3.13. Again, one noticeable exception to this is the considerable proportion of early retirees with household incomes below $10,000. Many of these respondents indicate they retired due to health problems, and their low incomes likely reflect a premature departure from the paid labour force.

Chart 3.13

Canadians Retired or Expecting to Retire Before Age 60, by Household Income, 1991

Household Income

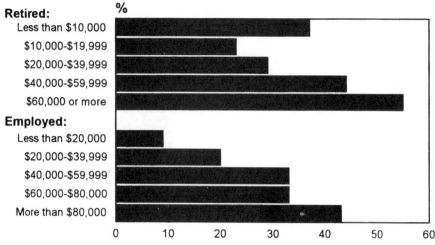

Source: Prepared by the Centre for International Statistics, using *Survey on Ageing and Independence* microdata, 1991.

Labour force status of spouse

The labour force status of one's spouse is also an important factor in the timing of retirement. As shown in Chart 3.14, expectations of early retirement are greatest among women with a husband employed full-time.[20] Such expectations are less prevalent where the husband is employed part-time, is unemployed or is not in the labour force at all. Among men, expectations of early retirement are similar among those with a wife employed full-time or part-time, but are much less prevalent where the wife is unemployed or out of the labour force.

This suggests that the financial uncertainty associated with an unemployed spouse diminishes expectations of early retirement. Conversely, the financial resources associated with a spouse (especially a husband) who is employed full-time appear to be positively associated with such expectations. And similarly, a greater number of employed family members within the household is positively associated with expectations of early retirement (especially among women), while the presence of one or more unemployed family members is negatively associated with such expectations.

32

Chart 3.14

Canadians Expecting to Retire Before Age 60, by Sex and Labour Force Status of Spouse, 1991

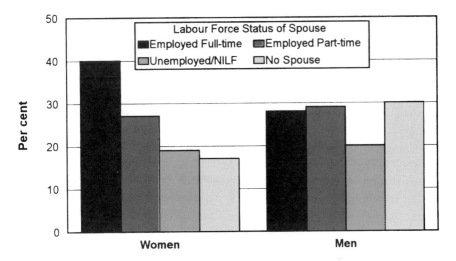

Source: Prepared by the Centre for International Statistics, using *Survey on Ageing and Independence* microdata, 1991.

Families with children

Because all of the respondents in the Survey on Ageing and Independence are 45 years of age and over (and half of them are age 65 and over), only a small proportion have children under 16 years of age living at home. A larger proportion have children between the ages of 16 and 24. Survey data indicate that among men between the ages of 55 and 64, those with children are less likely to be retired than those without. This suggests that children are a deterrent to retirement. However, evidence of this pattern is not as apparent among women.

These days, with people getting married and having children at later ages, the impact of children on the retirement decision is likely to become more important in the coming years.

Overall, the family context in which an individual lives has a considerable influence on the age that the person retires. The presence of a spouse, greater household income and two or more income earners is associated with retirement, or expectations of retirement, at earlier ages. This has been interpreted in terms of the economic security and resources mustered by the household, an interpretation reinforced by the fact that persons who own their home are more likely to retire early, or expect to retire early, than persons who rent. But, as will be documented in subsequent chapters, there are many "pathways" to retirement and not all people retiring early do so because of economic security. Some are pushed out of the labour force by job loss, poor health and other factors, and their early retirement is characterized by economic insecurity and uncertainty.

Age of Retirement and Health Factors

Studies which have included some consideration of health factors generally report a correlation between poor health and retirement at earlier ages.[21] However, there is a great deal of disagreement about this issue, revolving largely around the health measures used. Self-reported health measures, where respondents are asked to assess their health as either excellent, good, fair or poor, or to indicate whether their range of activities is limited by health problems, are most commonly used in retirement studies. Such measures are criticized on the grounds that they are based on the respondent's subjective interpretation of "poor" or "good" health. Moreover, such measures do not differentiate between actual and perceived health problems nor do they distinguish degrees of poor health or the severity of limitations to various activities. Consequently, two people who rate their health as poor might, in fact, have markedly different states of health. Concern also has been raised about whether indications of poor health by early retirees may represent *ex post facto* justifications for their early withdrawal from the labour force rather than the actual cause of their retirement decision.[22] Studies using alternative measures have produced mixed results.[23]

For some early retirees, "poor health" may merely be their own justification for leaving the work force.

Analysis of the Survey on Ageing and Independence illustrates these concerns. Three measures of health have been included in this analysis. In the first, respondents describe their health as excellent, good, fair or poor; in the second, respondents rank their health as either better, the same or worse than that of other people the same age; and finally, respondents indicate whether they are at all limited in activity because of a long-term illness, physical condition or health problem.

Analysis of actual and expected ages of retirement using these measures produces mixed results. Among retirees, the latter two measures indicate that poor health is associated with retirement at earlier ages, while the first measure indicates the opposite. Among working Canadians expecting to retire, the findings are very mixed. More than anything, the analysis highlights the limitations of self-reported health measures. Broad rankings of "excellent" or "poor" health, or subjective assessments of one's physical well-being compared to the wider population, are prone to error and likely to produce misleading results.

Uncertainty and the Retirement Transition

Up to this point, our analysis has focused on the actual and expected retirement ages of Canadians. However, many people are unable (or unwilling) to indicate the age at which they expect to retire. There are good reasons to include these people in this analysis. Some researchers argue that the potential for retirement uncertainty has increased in recent years. This has been attributed to the increasing unpredictability and uncertainty in the employment experiences of older workers, and to the shifting boundaries between retired and non-retired states.[24]

The noted European researcher Anne-Marie Guillemard argues that the social definition of "old age" is changing as people leave the labour force well before they begin to decline physically. And because of the growing discrepancy between the age of labour force exit and the age of public pension eligibility, welfare state institutions no longer serve as boundaries between the stages of people's lives. As Guillemard states: "Since the chronological markers are becoming less visible, the end of the life course has been blurred...The life course is becoming variable, imprecise, and contingent. As a result, workers can no longer predict at what age and under what conditions they will exit from work."[25]

Retirement uncertainties are expressed by many respondents in the Survey on Ageing and Independence. Those not already retired were asked to indicate the age at which they expect to do so. About one-quarter of those aged 45 to 54 said they didn't know. This is not surprising considering that retirement was 10 to 15 years in the future for many of these individuals. Yet even among respondents aged 55 to 64, more than one-fifth were uncertain about their plans.

Unfortunately, we have little data on the reasons underlying this uncertainty. It may arise because low income, inadequate retirement savings or potential job loss nurture doubts about one's ability to afford retirement. Alternatively, pension options, early retirement packages or flexible work arrangements may provide favourable choices regarding retirement and raise questions (and uncertainty) of a more positive nature. In short, Canadians who are unsure of their retirement plans may be so for many different reasons.

Nonetheless, for many Canadians, economic insecurity appears to be a principal underlying factor. As shown in Chart 3.15, non-retired Canadians in households with lower incomes are more likely to express retirement uncertainty than those with higher incomes. A similar pattern is evident when personal income is considered. Similarly, among non-retired Canadians, those with lower education levels, no employer-pension, and employment in semi-skilled and unskilled occupations are most likely to express uncertainty about their retirement. Again, these patterns support our explanation based on economic insecurity.

Chart 3.15

Employed Canadians: Per Cent Uncertain About Retirement Plans, by Age and Household Income, 1991

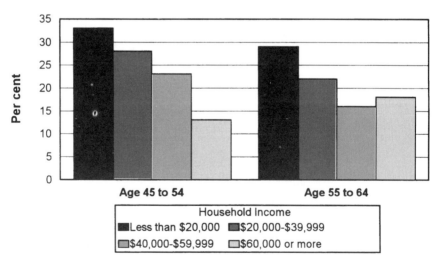

Source: Prepared by the Centre for International Statistics, using *Survey on Ageing and Independence* microdata, 1991.

The Road to Retirement

Because comparable data from previous years are not available, we cannot determine whether retirement uncertainty is more prevalent now than in the past. Nonetheless, it is clear that many Canadians are uncertain of their retirement intentions, and for many this uncertainty is associated with economic insecurity.

Canadians Who Will Not Retire

Most Canadians in the labour force eventually retire, but some do not. In 1993, there were approximately 74,000 Canadians aged 70 and over in the paid labour force. This represented 3.7 per cent of the total population in that age group.

Self-employed individuals are especially likely to remain in the labour force; 38 per cent of labour force participants aged 65 to 69 and 43 per cent of those aged 70 and over are self-employed, compared to only 9 per cent within the 25 to 44 age group and 10 per cent in the 45 to 54 age group. As noted earlier, the tendency of self-employed workers to defer or forego retirement may reflect their ability to adjust their work schedules to their liking or the economic insecurity they experience because of low incomes relative to paid employees.

Among employed respondents in the Survey on Ageing and Independence, 9 per cent of men and 10 per cent of women indicate they will not retire. The factors associated with the intention of not retiring are employment in the agricultural sector and lack of employer-pension coverage — two factors also associated with self-employment.

Conclusion

While age 65 may have been a prevalent reference point for retirement through the 1950s and 1960s, this is no longer the case. There exists tremendous variation in the range of actual and expected retirement ages. This has been interpreted as the destandardization of retirement. Individual circumstances and characteristics now play an increasingly important role in the retirement decision. While eligibility for public pensions no doubt remains a very important factor in this decision, it appears to be less so than in past years. Many more people now retire before becoming eligible for a public pension. For this reason, some writers have argued that public old age security programs no longer "regulate" the flow of people into retirement as they have in the past.[26]

Another implication of the destandardization of retirement is that there is a greater range of inequalities in Canadian society reflected in those making the retirement transition. Those with adequate resources, such as private pensions or retirement savings, may exercise control over the timing of their retirement, while those without such resources work on until they are eligible for a public pension or, as we will see in subsequent chapters, they are pushed out of the labour force by factors beyond their control. Trends that foster inequality, such as rising unemployment or increasing wage differences, are likely to be reflected in future patterns of retirement.

Along with the destandardization of retirement comes uncertainty. It is more and more difficult for people to foresee at what age and under what conditions they will leave the labour force, given the increasing range of choices and possibilities.[27] This uncertainty makes retirement planning increasingly difficult, but also increasingly important.

Our understanding of the life course is also being altered by the destandardization of retirement. As emphasized earlier, retirement no longer signals the onset of old age, nor is it demarcated by entry into the old age security system. Consequently, our conceptions of what it means to be retired and what it means to be old are changing.

This analysis has underscored the importance of family characteristics in the retirement transition. This importance will undoubtedly increase in the coming decades as a growing proportion of families are comprised of dual-earner couples. As will be shown in Chapter Five, spousal factors significantly influence retirement decisions. Consequently, retirement policies recognizing familial, as well as individual, characteristics will probably be the most effective.

This analysis also has suggested that factors associated with early retirement differ for men and women, for example, the influence of marital status and pension coverage on the timing of retirement. Similar results have been reported elsewhere.[28] Such gender variations may pose complications for policy-makers. For example, changes in pension legislation designed to encourage older workers to remain in, or leave, the labour force may have very different impacts on men and women.

CHAPTER 4 The Process of Retirement

With the decline in labour force participation rates of older workers, it is clear that the *timing* of retirement is changing. A second dimension of change is the *process* through which people move into retirement. Not only is this process being undertaken at a younger age, it is becoming more varied. This change has been conceptualized in two interrelated ways.

First, some researchers have emphasized the changing labour force activities of older workers *en route* to retirement. For example, some have emphasized rising joblessness and long-term unemployment as factors increasingly precipitating retirement.[1] Older workers facing long and possibly unsuccessful job searches often leave the labour force and become retired simply for lack of employment alternatives.

"Bridge jobs" have also been documented as a new pathway to retirement, bridging the gap between the end of career employment and the beginning of permanent retirement.[2] This is increasingly important as many older workers face the termination of a career job while still in their early to mid 50s.[3] Others may seek other types of "non-standard" employment, such as part-time and temporary jobs, as new pathways to retirement. These jobs may offer workers the potential for "partial" or "flexible" retirement by enabling them to gradually reduce their hours of work.[4]

A second way of looking at changes in the retirement process is in terms of financial arrangements. For example, Martin Kohli and his colleagues take as their starting point the increasing "gap" between the age at which workers exit the labour market and the age at which they are eligible for a public pension.[5] They ask the question: how are workers financially bridging this gap when they have neither earnings from employment nor income from public pensions? They argue that new institutional arrangements, including disability pensions, unemployment insurance, occupational pensions and "pre-retirement" programs, serve as pathways between work and entry into the old-age pension system.[6] Laczko and Phillipson identify a similar set of routes.[7]

Changes in the labour market, especially high unemployment, have greatly altered the ways Canadians retire today.

There is considerable overlap between the financial and labour market aspects of these pathways. Unemployment is a labour market status and unemployment insurance is a source of income — both may lead to retirement. For clarity's sake, however, analysis in this chapter is limited to changing labour market conditions and the impact of these changes on the retirement process. Unemployment, non-standard employment and "post-retirement" employment are examined, but detailed analysis of the financial pathways to retirement is presented in Chapter Six.

Unemployment as a Pathway to Retirement

Compared to the earlier post-war period, unemployment in Canada has worsened considerably in the past two decades. In the 1950s and 1960s, unemployment rates averaged less than 5 per cent. Through the 1970s, the rate averaged 6.7 per cent, rising to an average of 9.3 per cent through the 1980s. Between 1990 and 1993 it has remained high, averaging 10.2 per cent.[8] Older workers have been far from immune to rising joblessness. The unemployment rate among Canadians aged 45 to 64, like the rate for the

Chart 4.1

**Unemployment Rates by Sex and Age Groups
Canada 1975-1993**

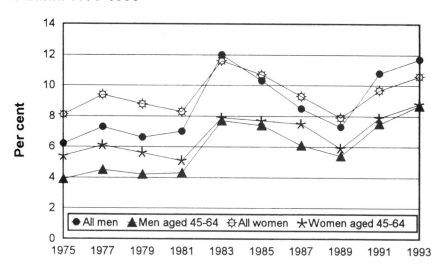

Source: Statistics Canada, *Labour Force Annual Averages*, Cat. 71-529, various years.

entire labour force, increased dramatically during recessionary periods (1981-82 and 1991-92). And in spite of the economic recovery of the late 1980s, the rates among older men did not return to their pre-recession levels.

To understand the impact of unemployment on the retirement transition, it is useful to consider the characteristics of unemployment among older workers. As shown in Chart 4.1, unemployment rates among these workers are lower than the labour force average, a fact attributable in part to their longer job tenure and greater job seniority. But, while older workers are less likely to become unemployed, those who do lose their jobs face particular difficulties finding new ones. As shown in Chart 4.2, the average duration of their unemployment is much longer than the overall labour force average.

This duration increased through the 1980s. For men over age 45, it rose from 18 weeks in 1976 to 32 weeks in 1985, declining slightly during the economic recovery of the latter 1980s. But by 1993 the average duration of unemployment among older men reached 35 weeks, while for those aged 15 to 24 it was 17 weeks.

It is also important to note that these figures probably underestimate the true scope of unemployment among older Canadians, since "discouraged workers" are not included in the data.

Chart 4.2

Unemployed Canadians: Average Duration of Unemployment by Age Groups, Selected Years

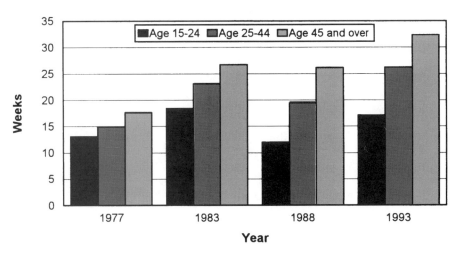

Source: Statistics Canada, *Labour Force Annual Averages*, Cat. 71-529, selected years.

Discouraged workers are individuals who have previously looked for a job, but have given up their search because they believe no jobs are available. As shown in Chart 4.3, older workers are particularly likely to be in this group.[9] So while official rates indicate older workers are less likely to be unemployed, they are more likely to face longer spells of unemployment and to become discouraged workers than their younger counterparts.

A critical question at this point is whether unemployment really is a path leading from the labour market into retirement. Considerable evidence suggests that it is. Ernest Akyeampong of Statistics Canada examined the circumstances of workers who were permanently laid off because of plant closures, work load reductions and similar reasons during the 1981-1984 recessionary period.[10] He found that only 39 per cent of workers aged 55 to 64 had found employment by 1986, compared to 65 per cent of workers aged 25 to 54. "Moreover, about 41 per cent of the older workers had left the labour force; only 14 per cent of the younger ones had done so."[11]

The recession of the early 1990s had a similar effect. During the 1990-1992 period, the number of workers who retired *earlier than planned* because of layoffs or plant closures (45,000) "...was

Chart 4.3

Discouraged Workers as a Per Cent of Total Unemployed by Age Group and Sex, Canada 1992

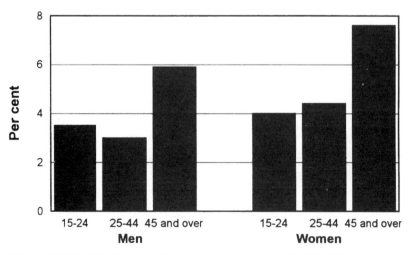

Source: Statistics Canada, *Labour Force Annual Averages*, Cat. 71-529, 1993.

more than double the number for the 1987-89 period (20,000)."[12] Again, the recession was particularly hard on older workers, with job loss and unemployment forcing many into retirement.

Frank Laczko also emphasizes the role of job loss in retirement, and adds an occupational dimension to this. He shows that British men in semi-skilled and unskilled occupations are "...disproportionately affected by the decline in older workers' employment opportunities," while men in managerial and other non-manual occupations are considerably less affected. Overall, he concludes, exit routes from employment to retirement vary substantially across social class.[13]

Analysis from the Survey of Consumer Finances lends credence to this position. Table 4.1 includes Canadians aged 55 to 64 who are not in the labour force (neither currently working nor looking for work), but who worked within the past five years. The table shows their previous occupation as well as the reason why they left the labour force. Of Canadians from professional and managerial occupations, 68 per cent said they retired, 13 per cent said they were laid off, and 19 per cent left for other reasons. In contrast, Canadians from other occupations are considerably less likely to state that they retired and far more apt to say they were laid off or left for other reasons. These estimates are similar for both men and women. It is not possible to determine whether these people intend to re-enter the labour force in the future, but given the difficulties unemployed older workers face in finding new jobs, it is likely many will remain jobless.

Table 4.1

Persons Aged 55 to 64 not in the Labour Force but Who Worked Within the Last Five Years: Reason for Leaving Last Job by Occupation, Canada 1991

Occupation of last job	Retired	Lost Job/ Laid Off	Other Reasons	Total
Professional/Managerial	68	13	19	100%
Sales/Service	42	23	35	100%
Clerical	45	32	23	100%
Blue Collar*	46	34	21	100%

*Includes farming, fishing, forestry, mining, construction trades, product fabricating and assembly, transport equipment operation, materials handling and other crafts and equipment operations. Sample size is too small to provide more detailed estimates.

Source: Prepared by the Centre for International Statistics using Survey of Consumer Finances microdata, 1992.

Prospects for the older unemployed worker in the coming years look gloomy. Despite forecasts of economic growth in Canada, the OECD predicts that unemployment rates will remain above 10 per cent. Increases in economic productivity are expected to come via technological change and corporate restructuring, rather than from more people returning to the work force.

Non-standard Employment and Retirement

The changing form of employment available to Canadian workers is another factor which may potentially transform the retirement process. Through much of the post-war period, the standard form of employment in Canada and other industrialized countries was the permanent, full-time, full-year job. While this is still the case for most Canadians,[14] an important change has been the emergence of "non-standard" employment — jobs that are neither permanent, nor full-time. The former Economic Council of Canada estimated that 44 per cent of all new jobs created during the 1980s were non-standard.[15] By 1989, one-fifth of working-age Canadians were employed in part-time, part-year and temporary jobs.[16]

While many non-standard jobs are held by young workers, 16 per cent of employed men and 30 per cent of employed women aged 55 to 64 work in part-time, part-year and temporary jobs.

Non-standard employment may provide a welcome new pathway to retirement, affording older workers greater opportunity to gradually reduce their hours of work and to move into retirement step-by-step. This would give workers a less costly alternative to complete retirement and would ease their transition out of the labour force. There is some evidence suggesting that such arrangements are preferred by older workers.[17] Partial or gradual retirement would also enable employers to keep highly skilled and experienced workers on the job at least part-time, so that they could pass on their skills and expertise to younger workers.

In fact, the data suggest that, while on the rise, the use of non-standard employment as a pathway to retirement is still not very prevalent. In the Survey on Ageing and Independence, retired respondents were asked if they changed their work patterns (for example, worked part-time or worked more hours) in preparation for retirement. Only 14 per cent of retirees indicated they had done so. Some occupational differences are noticeable, with 20 per cent of retirees from professional and managerial positions changing their work patterns, compared to only 10 per cent of those from unskilled positions. Between these extremes, occupational variations are not marked. Of the employed respondents expecting to retire, 15 per cent indicated they had changed, or were currently changing, their work patterns in preparation for retirement.

In his study of labour force withdrawal among older workers, Lars Osberg reached a similar conclusion, finding that very few workers reduce their hours of work in preparation for retirement. He states: "There is little evidence of a gradual 'tailing off' of hours of work as people age and a good deal of evidence that the transition is usually fairly abrupt — from full-time employment to unemployment or not in the labour force."[18]

Even so, evidence from the Labour Force Survey indicates there has been an increase in the rate of part-time employment among older workers. As shown in Table 4.2, the rate of part-time employment among men aged 55 to 64 more than doubled between 1981 and 1993, rising from 3 to 7 per cent. The rate also increased among older women. Within this age group, the most frequently cited reason for part-time employment was simply that a full-time job was not wanted. This was indicated by 48 per cent of older men and 64 per cent of older women in 1993. The second most frequently cited reason was that a full-time job couldn't be found, indicated by 41 and 27 per cent of men and women respectively.

While these figures are not direct measures of changes in work patterns made in preparation for retirement, they do indicate that a growing proportion of older workers are voluntarily reducing their work hours. This provides some support for the view that more and more older workers are opting for a gradual transition into retirement via part-time employment. But again, the relatively small share of older workers, particularly men, employed on a part-time basis suggests that this is still a relatively untrodden pathway to retirement.

Table 4.2

Employed Men and Women Aged 55 to 64: Per Cent Employed Part -Time, Canada, Selected Years

	1981	1986	1993
Men	3	5	7
Women	25	28	30

Source: Statistics Canada, *Labour Force Annual Averages 1975-1983* ,*Labour Force Annual Averages 1981-1988*, Cat. 71-529 and *Labour Force Annual Averages 1993*, Cat. 71-220.

Considerable attention has been paid to the use of flexible schedules as a way to enable people with children to balance employment and family responsibilities. Such schedules, although not a non-standard form of employment, are also worth considering in the retirement transition. A flexible work schedule "...exists when an employee is allowed to vary, within certain limits, the beginning and end of the workday."[19] Such arrangements, of course, may also be used to accumulate additional work hours which can be taken as leave at a later date.

Flexible work hours may be a way to provide older workers with more options in the retirement transition, altering or reducing their hours of work rather than "punching the clock" at 8 a.m. and 5 p.m. Yet, in fact, few older workers are employed with such an arrangement. As shown in Table 4.3, 13 per cent of men aged 55 to 64 work on a "flexitime" schedule, while the overall average for men is 15.6 per cent. Older women are somewhat more likely to work flexible hours.

While non-standard forms of employment may open new and more flexible pathways to retirement, there is a more pessimistic interpretation of these developments. Many non-standard jobs pay poorer wages, offer fewer benefits and provide less stable employment than full-time permanent positions. Consequently, the Economic Council of Canada reports: "...the increase in non-standard jobs may be increasing the economic insecurity of growing numbers of workers."[20] Results from the Survey on Ageing and Independence confirm some of these more negative aspects. Of working Canadians over 45 years of age, almost 60 per cent employed in full-time, full-year jobs have employer-pension coverage (see Table 4.4). In contrast, this is the case for only about one-quarter to one-third of part-time and part-year workers.

Because of the lower rate of pension coverage in non-standard jobs, one consequence of the rise of these kinds of employment will be an increase in the number of Canadian workers depending on government programs (such as CPP/QPP and OAS) as their primary

Table 4.3

Paid Employees Working on Flexible Schedules, by Age Group and Sex, Canada 1991 (per cent)

	Men	Women
All	16	17
15 to 24	11	12
25 to 44	18	19
45 to 54	14	15
55 to 64	13	18

Source: Prepared by the Centre for International Statistics using Survey of Work Arrangements microdata, 1991.

source of retirement income. However, even these public sources of income may be out of reach for some workers.

To be eligible to contribute to Canada/Quebec Pension Plans (CPP/QPP), a worker's annual earnings must exceed a minimum amount known as the "Year's Basic Exemption" (YBE). In 1990, 14 per cent of part-time jobs fell below this minimum and hence were excluded from the plan.[21] The largest share of these jobs were held by people in their teens and early 20s, but many were also held by persons, especially women, aged 25 and over. And many of these women had more than a passing attachment to the labour force, occupying these CPP/QPP ineligible jobs for several years. So despite extensive participation in the paid labour force, some workers in non-standard jobs are excluded from the economic security derived from ongoing participation in either private or public pension programs.

In this context, it is not surprising perhaps that workers in non-standard jobs are more likely to defer retirement to later ages, and are also more likely to express uncertainty regarding their expected age of retirement. Moreover, compared to full-time/full-year workers, Canadians in part-time and part-year jobs are less likely to expect their household income to be sufficient for their retirement. Given these factors, the growing number of workers in non-standard jobs are likely to face a more difficult transition into retirement than those with the benefits of permanent full-time employment.

Perhaps most importantly, a move to part-time or part-year employment is likely to involve severe long-term financial penalties for older workers since pension entitlements and severance packages

Table 4.4

Employed Canadians Age 45 and Over: Type of Employment by Selected Characteristics, Canada 1991

	% with employer - pension	% uncertain of retirement age	% expecting to retire before age 60	% think income adequate to retire as planned
Full-time/ Full-year	58	22	31	66
Part-time	25	32	23	58
Part-year	34	28	17	60

Source: Prepared by the Centre for International Statistics using Survey on Ageing and Independence microdata, 1991.

are generally calculated on the basis of the worker's final years in the labour force. A move to part-time employment, with its consequent drop in pay, is likely to result in a reduction in future retirement income. Consequently, workers who may be willing to reduce their work hours and exchange current earnings for greater leisure time, may still be unwilling to undertake part-time or part-year employment because of longer-term financial penalties.

The same issue confronts other work arrangements, such as job sharing and the four-day workweek. People approaching retirement may be reluctant to undertake such employment because of the long-term financial consequences. Likewise, under current arrangements, people in their 30s and 40s would face reduced pension entitlements (both public and private) if work sharing and the four-day workweek were pursued as measures to combat unemployment. Changes to pension provisions would be necessary if these forms of employment were to be implemented without imposing longer-term costs on workers.

The self-employed worker

Up to this point, the discussion has focused primarily on paid employees. However, a growing number of Canadians are "becoming their own boss." Self-employment is on the rise after many decades of decline. As shown in Table 4.5, the number of self-employed workers in Canada grew by 89 per cent between 1975 and 1993. The number of paid employees grew by only 28 per cent. Several factors may be contributing to this trend, including the introduction of new technologies, labour cost advantages gained by small firms in recent years, new employment arrangements implemented by large firms, and the growth of service industries.

Table 4.5

Employment by Class of Worker , Canada 1975 - 1993

	Number of Workers (000s)			Per cent Change		
	1975	1986	1993	1975-1986	1986-1993	1975-1993
Paid Employees	8,142	9,979	10,399	22.6%	4.2%	27.7%
Self-employed	1,011	1,556	1,912	53.9%	22.9%	89.1%

Source: Prepared by the Centre for International Statistics using Gary Cohen, *Enterprising Canadians: The Self-Employed in Canada*. Statistics Canada, Cat.71-536, and *Labour Force Annual Averages 1993*. Statistics Canada Cat. 71-220.

The Road to Retirement

The labour force profile of older workers is being changed by this shift. Among employed men aged 55 to 64, for example, the proportion who were self-employed rose from 21 per cent in 1975 to 32 per cent in 1992 (see Table 4.6). Among employed women in this age group, the proportion who were self-employed rose from 9 to 15 per cent.

Part of this increase reflects the greater tendency of self-employed workers to defer retirement. As a growing number of paid employees in older age groups take early retirement and leave the labour force, a rising proportion of the workers who remain in it are self-employed. However, this is not the entire story, because more and more workers are leaving paid employment to start their own businesses.

This trend has a number of implications. The trend towards early retirement may be diminished somewhat, since self-employed individuals are more likely than paid employees to remain in the labour force until older ages. Moreover, many people who return to the labour force after their initial retirement do so on a self-employed basis. Self-employed workers are also more likely to rely on private investments, such as Registered Retirement Savings Plans (RRSPs), rather than employer-pensions for their retirement income. This will likely increase utilization of the RRSP program and may also fuel demands for increases in maximum contribution limits. Lastly, wide variations in the characteristics of self-employment are evident across industry sectors and are likely to be reflected in the retirement transition. For example, as shown in Table 4.7, self-employment earnings

Table 4.6

Per Cent of Employed Labour Force Comprised of Self-Employed Workers, by Age Group and Sex, Canada 1975 - 1992

	Men			Women		
	1975	1986	1992	1975	1986	1992
All	14	17	20	6	8	10
15 to 24	4	5	6	4	6	8
25 to 44	14	16	18	5	8	9
45 to 54	20	24	24	7	11	13
55 to 64	21	26	32	9	13	15
65 & over	38	56	61	23	26	27

Source: Prepared by the Centre for International Statistics using Gary Cohen, *Enterprising Canadians: The Self-Employed in Canada*. Statistics Canada, Cat.71-536 and Survey of Consumer Finances microdata, 1993.

Table 4.7

Earnings of Self-Employed and Paid Workers in Personal Household and Related Services and Business Services, Canada 1985

	Personal, Household & Related Services	Business Services
	($)	($)
All Self Employed		
median earnings	5,100	29,700
average earnings	10,700	37,200
Self-Employed with No Paid Employees		
median earnings	3,300	19,600
average earnings	8,600	27,200
Self-Employed with Paid Employees		
median earnings	17,600	37,400
average earnings	19,600	43,400
All Paid Employees		
median earnings	10,400	16,800
average earnings	12,800	20,400

Source: Gary Cohen, *Enterprising Canadians: The Self-Employed in Canada*. Statistics Canada, Cat.71-536, 1988.

in personal, household and related services are only a fraction of those in business services (two sectors where self-employment has grown very rapidly). Retirement preparations are likely to be difficult for individuals in the former industries given their low average earnings, while those in business services and other more profitable sectors are much more likely to be able to make RRSP contributions and other retirement preparations.

Returning to the Labour Force

The transition into retirement does not always imply a complete withdrawal from paid employment. Retired respondents in the Survey on Ageing and Independence were asked: "After you retired, did you ever go back to work at any job or employment?" Of the retirees over the age of 45, 17 per cent had returned to work, while 83 per cent had not. Post-retirement work patterns very significantly between the sexes. The proportion of male retirees returning to paid labour (21 per cent) is almost twice that of female retirees (11 per cent).

Not unexpectedly, Canadians who return to paid labour after their initial retirement are likely to have retired somewhat earlier than those who remain out of the labour force. This is especially the case with women. Among women, 48 per cent of "returners" retired at less than 60 years of age compared to 37 per cent of "non-returners" (see Table 4.8). Similarly, among retired men, returners are more likely to have initially retired before age 60.

There is also a correlation between the type of work individuals did prior to retirement and their possible post-retirement re-entry into the labour force. Generally speaking, the higher an individual's skill or managerial level, the greater the likelihood of that person returning to the work force after retirement. A relatively large proportion of men employed in professional and senior management occupations returned to paid labour at some point after retirement (40 per cent), a proportion considerably higher than in any other occupational group. Men employed in semi-skilled and unskilled occupations prior to retirement are the least likely to return to paid labour.

The influence of occupation on women's post-retirement re-entry into the labour force is quite different from that of men. In almost every occupational group, the proportion of retired women who return to paid labour is between 9 and 15 per cent. Women from no single occupational group stand out as most likely to return to paid labour after retirement, the only exception being that women from unskilled occupations are unlikely to do so.

The survey does not provide information on the occupations or industries in which these individuals find employment after retirement (i.e. only data on occupation and industry prior to retirement were collected). Consequently, the extent to which post-retirement employment constitutes a "career-shift" remains to be explored.

Table 4.8
Age of Initial Retirement Among Retirees Returning and Not Returning to Paid Employment, by Sex, Canada 1991

	Less than 59	60-64	65	66 or over	Total
Men					
Returners	33	28	26	14	100%
Non-Returners	26	34	29	12	100%
Women					
Returners	48	32	13	7	100%
Non-Returners	37	31	20	12	100%

Source: Prepared by the Centre for International Statistics using Survey on Ageing and Independence microdata, 1991.

Most post-retirement employment is part-time. This is the case for 76 per cent of male returners and 88 per cent of female returners; data are not available to determine whether this is voluntary or not. Overall, the higher rate of post-retirement employment among men and their lower rate of part-time work suggests that, compared to retired women, men are more likely to retain a greater attachment to the labour force.

Of those undertaking post-retirement employment, almost three-quarters work for a different employer than the one they worked for prior to retirement. Many also become self-employed, with almost one in four men and one in five women doing so.

Motivations for returning to work cannot be imputed to these survey respondents because the appropriate information is not available. However, their reasons for retirement can be examined and comparisons drawn between retirees who have and have not returned to work. Two noticeable differences stand out (see Chart 4.4). First, retirees who return to work are less likely to have

Chart 4.4

Reasons for Retirement Among Retirees Returning and Not Returning to Paid Employment, Canada 1991

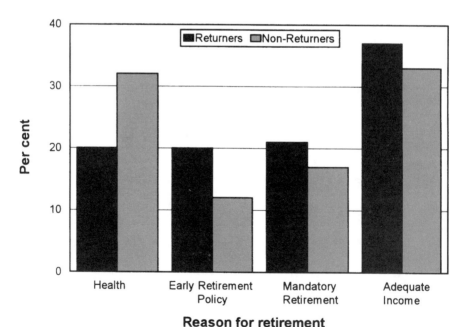

Source: Prepared by the Centre for International Statistics, using *Survey on Ageing and Independence* microdata, 1991.

The Road to Retirement

retired for health reasons compared to those who do not return (20 per cent versus 32 per cent respectively). And second, a larger proportion of returners cite early retirement plans (20 per cent). There are other differences, although these are insignificant, ranging from 3 to 4 percentage points. (A more detailed discussion of reasons for retirement is presented in Chapter Five.)

Because comparable historical data are not available, it cannot be determined whether or not post-retirement employment is on the rise. When comparisons are drawn across retirees in different age groups, however, little variation is evident. Similar proportions of retirees in both younger and older age groups indicate they return to paid employment at some point. This suggests that post-retirement has remained stable over time. However, in light of the general trend towards early retirement and the fact that men and women who retire at younger ages are most likely to return to employment, one might speculate that an upward trend in post-retirement employment will emerge in the coming years.

Conclusion

Changes in the labour market have altered the avenues through which Canadians enter retirement. Persistently high rates of unemployment have been especially significant in this regard. Although older workers are less likely to lose their jobs than their younger counterparts, once they are unemployed, older workers face particular difficulties finding new employment. Evidence suggests that, for some Canadians, retirement is "disguised unemployment," as workers opt to leave the labour market rather than face the prospects of a long, and possibly fruitless, job search. Compared to the 1960s, when the unemployment rate among older workers was well below five per cent, this is a new development.

To address this situation, one policy question to be considered is whether public programs for older workers are designed to compensate them for lost jobs or re-integrate them into the labour force. In most European countries, the tendency has been toward compensation rather than integration, with Sweden being the only notable exception.[22] The situation is similar in Canada. One of the few programs for older workers, the Program for Older Worker Adjustment (POWA), provides compensation to unemployed workers aged 55 to 64 after Unemployment Insurance and other normal assistance programs have run out.[23] Programs for re-integration have been sparse, and older workers have traditionally been excluded from retraining programs in Canada.[24] With persistently high rates of unemployment, the need for re-integration is pressing. The fact that many older workers persist in their job searches for prolonged periods suggests that they are eager to remain in the labour force and would be receptive to retraining and re-employment programs.

It is also important to consider unemployment in discussions of CPP/QPP eligibility. The option of raising the age of eligibility has been mentioned in policy discussions, largely because of concerns over the financial viability of CPP/QPP. This would impose severe financial hardships on older workers. Many are denied access to market earnings, and the withdrawal of public pensions would eliminate one of the few alternatives left to them. The probable result would be the depletion of their personal savings, a reliance on social assistance (welfare) and, in general, an increase in poverty among older Canadians.

The growth of part-time and other forms of non-standard employment offers the potential to transform the retirement transition. However, it appears only a small proportion of older workers are changing their work patterns in preparation for retirement. Because pensions and severance packages are often based on earnings in previous years, workers are likely to face financial penalties for reducing their hours and earnings prior to retirement. Steps to eliminate these penalties would make partial retirement a more viable option. Efforts to improve the quality of non-standard jobs would also improve the retirement options available to Canadians. Extending pension coverage to all temporary and part-time workers would be an important first step in this direction.

CHAPTER 5 The Reasons for Retirement

In the previous two chapters, the importance of demographic, labour market and other factors in the retirement transition were considered. The more subjective aspects of this transition were not captured, however. If asked why they retired before age 60, for example, people are unlikely to respond that it was because of their level of education or their job tenure. They are more likely to say they retired because of adequate income, health factors, early retirement policies or other reasons. These *stated* reasons are the subject of this chapter.

In many respects, these reasons reflect broader demographic and economic trends, and provide further insights on the various pathways to retirement. For example, the growing importance of early retirement policies (where employees are offered financial incentives or early pension plan eligibility) as a mechanism for work force adjustment is confirmed by the growing number of people who cite such policies as influential factors in their retirement. Likewise, the high rate of unemployment among older workers is reflected in the fact that many cite a lack of work as their reason for retirement. Overall, these stated reasons provide insight into the subjective dimensions of retirement as well as the broader economic picture.

Involuntary early retirement is most prevalent among people who can least afford it.

As noted in earlier chapters, there is tremendous diversity in the retirement transition. This is an important theme in the first half of this chapter, in which we look at the reasons for retirement among different socio-economic groups, among men and women, among different age groups within the retired population, and finally among Canadians already retired compared to those expecting to retire. In the second half of the chapter, we look at voluntary versus involuntary retirement.

Respondents in the Survey on Ageing and Independence were given a list of possible reasons for retirement and asked to select all those applicable to them. As Chart 5.1 shows, the desire to stop working is the most common reason, cited by 56 per cent of retired Canadians. The second most frequently cited reason is having adequate retirement income (34 per cent) followed closely by health reasons (30 per cent). Other reasons are mentioned much less often. Mandatory retirement policies are reported by 18 per cent of retirees and early retirement policies by 14 per cent. Less than one in ten retirees mention the need to provide care to a family member, lack of work, or pressure from co-workers.

Overall, the data confirm that most people want to retire as early as possible and do so as soon as they can afford to. On the other hand, those forced into retirement by health factors, mandatory retirement policies and so on, though proportionally fewer, still account for 465,000 Canadians.

Differences Across Socio-Economic Status

In his study of why people in Britain leave the labour force, Frank Laczko concludes "it is clear that the pattern of exit from the labour market varies substantially according to social class...." [1] For Laczko, social class is defined primarily in terms of occupation, which is related to education and income. Evidence from the Survey on Ageing and Independence points to a similar conclusion, illustrating the diverse pathways taken by people of different socio-economic status.

Chart 5.1

Reasons for Retirement Cited by Retired Canadians, 1991

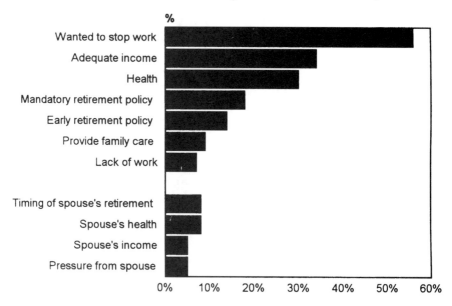

Source: Prepared by the Centre for International Statistics, using *Survey on Ageing and Independence* microdata, 1991.

The Road to Retirement

Adequate retirement income

The starkest contrast between socio-economic groups is evident when retirement motivated by whether or not one has the adequate income is considered. As shown in Table 5.1, men and women from professional, managerial and technical occupations are much more likely to cite adequate income as a reason for retirement than those in semi-skilled and unskilled occupations. Retirees who have higher levels of income and education are also more likely to cite adequacy of income as a motivating factor (see Appendix 5.1 for data on all retirement reasons by occupation, education and income). Among persons still in the labour force the same patterns are evident; persons with higher levels of income and education, and from professional and managerial occupations, are much more likely to cite adequacy of income as an expected reason for their approaching retirement (see Appendix 5.2).

Table 5.1

Retired Canadians: Selected Reasons for Retirement by Sex, Occupation and Personal Income 1991 (per cent)

	Adequate Income	Lack of Work	Early Retirement Policies	Health
Men				
Professional/Senior Mgmt.	48	5	24	19
Semi-Prof./Tech./Mid-Mgmt.*	55	5	23	22
Supervisory/Skilled	39	4	19	29
Semi-Skilled/Unskilled	31	9	15	33
Women				
Professional/Senior Mgmt.	44	1	17	20
Semi-Prof./Tech./Mid-Mgmt.*	31	6	8	20
Supervisory/Skilled	29	8	5	23
Semi-Skilled/Unskilled	20	9	5	34
Men				
Less than $10,000	18	12	3	51
$10,000 - $19,999	26	9	10	37
$20,000 - $39,999	48	3	23	26
$40,000 or more	63	2	36	15
Women				
Less than $10,000	14	11	3	39
$10,000 - $19,999	28	6	10	27
$20,000 - $39,999	45	3	8	22
$40,000 or more	()	()	()	()

* Includes semi-professional, technical and middle management occupations.
() Sample includes size too small to provide reliable estimates.

Source Prepared by the Centre for International Statistics using Survey on Ageing and Independence microdata, 1991.

Lack of work

The differing impact of unemployment is evident across income, education and occupation. Among retirees and especially among employed persons expecting to retire, those from unskilled and semi-skilled occupations are much more likely to cite lack of work as a retirement reason. Among persons in the labour force, 22 per cent of men and 29 per cent of women employed in semi-skilled and unskilled occupations mention this as an expected reason for their retirement (see Appendix 5.2). This reinforces the evidence in Chapter Four documenting joblessness as an increasingly prevalent pathway for older workers.

Lack of work is also associated with lower levels of education and income. The relationship between unemployment and low income may flow in two directions. Persons in semi-skilled and unskilled occupations (earning low wages) may be especially vulnerable to job loss resulting from technological innovations, lulls in consumer demand and so on. On the other hand, unemployment prior to retirement may involve depleting one's savings and a loss of pension contributions, and consequently, a low income in retirement. In either case, individuals entering retirement via unemployment are more vulnerable to impoverishment in later life and are more likely to be dependent upon public pensions.[2]

Early retirement policies

Variation across socio-economic status is also evident when early retirement policies are considered. These policies include financial incentives and early eligibility for employer-pension benefits designed to encourage older workers to leave their jobs. Retired and employed Canadians with high incomes, high levels of education, and professional and managerial employment are the most likely to cite the importance of such policies for retirement. Workers at the other end of the financial, educational and occupational spectrum are least likely.

Health

Socio-economic indicators are also associated with health as a reason for retirement. Again, lower levels of income and education, and "blue-collar" employment are positively associated with retirement due to health factors. The link between occupation and poor health has been well-established elsewhere,[3] and we might propose that job-related injuries or physical demands of many blue-collar jobs may not only be a reason for retiring but also a factor in poor health later in life.

Overall, it is clear that people from different socio-economic levels retire for different reasons. Those at the bottom of the spectrum are more likely than those at the top to cite lack of work and health factors as reasons for retirement, and less likely to cite adequacy of income and early retirement policies. When the analysis is limited to early retirement, these differences are even more striking.

Diversity across socio-economic status does not tell the whole story, however. Gender differences in the home and the labour market are also reflected in the reasons for retirement.

Differences Between Men and Women

As has long been observed, the labour force characteristics of men and women differ considerably. For example, in 1992, 26 per cent of women worked in part-time jobs compared to 9 per cent of men; in fact, women comprise about 70 per cent of the part-time labour force. In occupational terms, men are distributed relatively evenly across occupational categories, while women are more concentrated in a few.[4] Women are also less likely to be covered by an employer-pension plan and to be unionized.[5] Research has also shown that women undertake a dual role, working in both the home and the labour force. Two Canadian sociologists, Wallace Clement and John Myles, have documented the consequences of this dual role, showing that women face more career disruptions and employment limitations than men because of child care and domestic labour responsibilities.[6] These differences are reflected in the reasons for retirement cited by men and women.

Adequate retirement income

Men are much more likely than women to retire early because they have an adequate retirement income. Of all retirees, 38 per cent of men and 27 per cent of women indicate that adequate income was a reason for their retirement (see Chart 5.2). This difference is also evident, although to a lesser extent, among men and women expecting to retire.

On average, given that an employed woman earns approximately 60 cents for every dollar earned by a man, this difference in retirement motivation is not surprising.[7] Some writers have suggested that changes to pension legislation and women's growing labour force participation have led to improvements in the financial security of retiring women.[8] Nonetheless, these improvements are not likely to benefit all women; those with sporadic employment or low paying, marginal jobs are likely to continue to experience financial insecurity.

Early retirement policies

Women are much less likely to retire because of early retirement policies. Among all retirees, 18 per cent of men and only 7 per cent of women indicate that such policies were an important factor in deciding to retire. Among early retirees (before age 60), 33 per cent of men and 9 per cent of women say such policies were important. This finding is confirmed by the Labour Force Survey (LFS). In a recent supplement to the LFS, respondents who retired earlier than expected were asked whether they received an incentive payment or "cashout" in addition to their regular retirement benefits. Of these retirees, 30 per cent of the men, but only 12 per cent of the women, received such an incentive.[9]

Evidence suggests it is the prevalence of part-time employment among women that accounts for some of this difference. That is, part-time workers, seven in ten of whom are women, are much less likely to mention the importance of early retirement policies than those employed full-time.

Family care

The need to provide family care is a much greater factor in the retirement experience for women than men. Thirteen per cent of all retired women say that the need to provide family care was a motivating factor in their retirement; this is cited by only five per cent of retired men. It is interesting to note that among women, the prevalence of this reason varies across income level. Retired and employed women with higher levels of income and education are less likely to cite the provision of family care as an actual or expected reason for retirement than those with lower levels. This may be because it is more economical for women with higher incomes to purchase such care on the market rather than give up their paid employment in order to provide it themselves.

Overall, the prevalence of family care as a retirement reason underscores women's joint responsibilities for paid work and domestic labour. Policies designed to alleviate the strains arising from this dual role would no doubt affect the lives of many working women.

Spousal factors

Finally, the presence of one's spouse more strongly affects the retirement decision of women than of men. The most important spousal factor for women is the timing of their husband's retirement; one in five married women indicate this was an important factor in their own retirement decision. Fewer women cite their spouse's health, the adequacy of their spouse's income, and pressure from their spouse as reasons for their own retirement. Fewer than one in twenty men cite spouse-related reasons for retirement.

Striking differences are also evident among employed women and men who expect to retire (see Chart 5.3). Of married women, almost half cite the timing of their spouse's retirement as a factor in their own retirement. This is the case for only 13 per cent of men. Spouse's health and income are also cited by much larger proportions of women than men.

These data indicate that the retirement plans of women are much more contingent on other family members than the plans of men. This is consistent with other analyses of gender differences in paid

Chart 5.2

Selected Reasons for Retirement Cited by Retired Men and Women, Canada 1991

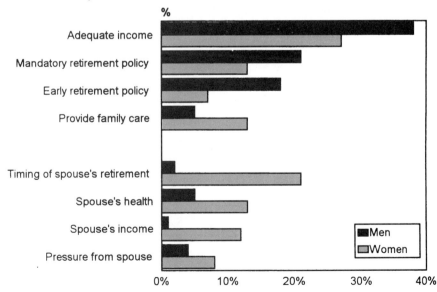

Source: Prepared by the Centre for International Statistics, using *Survey on Ageing and Independence* microdata, 1991.

Chart 5.3

Anticipated Reasons for Retirement Cited by Men and Women Expecting to Retire, Canada 1991

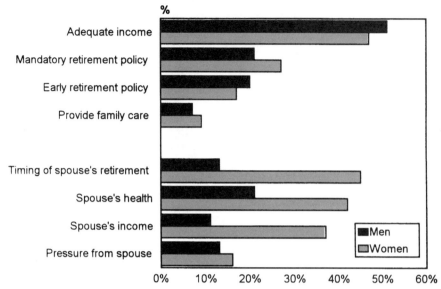

Source: Prepared by the Centre for International Statistics, using *Survey on Ageing and Independence* microdata, 1991.

employment. For example, Clement and Myles report that women are more likely than men to have been prevented from accepting a job, from looking for a job, from accepting a job transfer, or from accepting a promotion because of household or family responsibilities.[10] This is attributed to the fact that in most families the man's job is still the primary job and "women must do the adjusting." This imbalance is supported by wage inequalities between the sexes, which provide men with greater economic clout within the household. It is also reinforced by traditional views that child care, housework, care giving and other domestic roles are "naturally" the responsibility of women. In this context, perhaps it is not surprising that wives are more likely to adjust their retirement plans to fit their husband's rather than vice versa.

Trends in the Reasons for Retirement

In this study of retirement, an important issue to be explored is whether the picture portrayed in our findings is changing over time. For policy purposes, it would be helpful to know whether changes

The Road to Retirement

are taking place in the reasons for retirement. Unfortunately, the Survey on Ageing and Independence is a one-time snapshot taken in 1991, and there are no comparable predecessor studies.

The Survey does allow for two methods of approximating longitudinal trends. One is to compare different age groups within the retired population. To a limited extent, the characteristics of the younger age groups, compared with older age groups, approximate inter-generational change which may be taking place. One limitation of this strategy is that only a small proportion of respondents in younger age categories are retired. For example, only 5 per cent of Survey respondents aged 45 to 59 have retired, while the vast majority remain in the labour force. It is unlikely the retirement reasons listed by this 5 per cent are representative of the total age group, most of whom have yet to retire. In contrast, 83 per cent of Survey respondents aged 65 to 69 have retired, and conclusions drawn from this age group are far more reliable and representative.

To compensate for this limitation, reasons for retirement within age groups have been calculated separately for those respondents who retired before age 65. This reduces the influence of variations in retirement age and facilitates a clearer assessment of longitudinal trends. Nonetheless, comparisons drawn across age categories should still be interpreted with caution.

Using this method of approximation, results from the Survey on Ageing and Independence indicate that there are several trends in reasons for retirement (see Table 5.2). First, retirees in younger age groups are more likely than those in older ones to have retired because of early retirement policies, illustrating the growing popularity of these programs. This is particularly the case for men: of those retiring before age 65, 39 per cent aged 60 to 64 cite early retirement policies as a retirement reason compared to 18 per cent aged 75 and over. The OECD also emphasizes the growing prevalence of such policies.[12]

Second, women in younger age groups are more likely to have retired because of adequate retirement income than women in older age groups. This confirms the findings of Diane Galarneau at Statistics Canada, who documents an improvement in the financial position of women facing retirement. This improvement is attributable, in part, to changes in legislation extending pension coverage to part-time workers and to increasing labour force participation.[13] Among men the importance of adequacy of retirement income is less clear across age groups.

Third, there appears to be a trend towards a larger proportion of women in younger age groups retiring because of health factors. However, the incidence of death among older age groups may influence this pattern, since early retirees in older age groups who retired for health reasons are more likely to have died than early retirees in younger age groups. Because we are dealing only with survivors, the effect of this cannot be estimated. Moreover, as noted in Chapter Two, concerns have been expressed over the reliability of self-reported health measures. However, it may be suggested that as women take on the high-stress jobs previously in the domain of men, they may begin to suffer from the related health problems.

The other method of approximating longitudinal trends is to compare the characteristics of the retired population (who are also predominantly older) to the characteristics of Canadians still in the labour force who expect to retire (and who are predominantly younger). Using this method, three differences are found among men: those expecting to retire are more likely than those already retired to mention adequacy of income, lack of work and spousal factors as reasons. Similar patterns are found among women.

High expectations regarding adequacy of income suggests that many Canadians who are still in the labour force have confidence in their financial ability to retire. But, considering that retirement expec-

Table 5.2

Persons Who Retired Before Age 65: Selected Reasons for Retirement by Sex and Current Age, Canada 1991 (per cent)

	Early Retirement Policies	Adequate Retirement Income	Health
Men			
60 to 64	39	46	36
65 to 69	22	38	39
70 to 74	23	48	38
75 & over	18*	39	39
Women			
60 to 64	()	32	36
65 to 69	()	29	39
70 to 74	()	29	29
75 & over	()	26	29

* Estimate less reliable due to small sample size.
() Sample size too small to provide reliable estimates.

Source: Prepared by the Centre for International Statistics using Survey on Ageing and Independence microdata, 1991.

The Road to Retirement

tations and plans often remain unfulfilled, [14] reality may interfere with this confidence and force some to work longer than they expected or to retire on less. Lack of work as an increasingly prevalent reason for retirement underscores the uncertainty faced by many older workers in the current climate of recession and restructuring, and supports our earlier discussion of unemployment as a pathway into retirement. And finally, the increasing prevalence of spousal factors in the retirement decision attests to the growth of dual-earner families.

A number of other differences are found between women who are already retired and those expecting to retire, with the latter more likely to mention health factors, early retirement policies and mandatory retirement policies as influences. One might suggest that as the labour market experiences of younger women become broader — that is, as they enter industries and occupations from which they were previously excluded — the range of factors influencing their retirement decision will increase. For example, as women gain greater access to professional and senior managerial positions, more of them are likely to be influenced by early retirement and mandatory retirement policies.

Table 5.3
Actual and Expected Reasons for Retirement, by Sex, Canada 1991

| | Men | | Women | |
	Retired	Expect to Retire	Retired	Expect to Retire
Want to stop working	54	63	58	69
Adequate retirement income	38	51	27	47
Health	32	31	29	38
Mandatory retirement policy	21	21	13	27
Early retirement policy	18	20	7	17
Lack of work	6	15	7	22
Provide family care	5	7	13	9
Timing of spouses retirement	2	21	13	45
Spouse's health	5	13	21	42
Spouse's income	1	12	11	37
Pressure from spouse	4	8	13	16

Source: Prepared by the Centre for International Statistics using Survey on Ageing and Independence microdata, 1991.

The Retirement Decision: Voluntary or Involuntary

An important issue we need to consider in this analysis is whether retirement is voluntary or involuntary. Are Canadians leaving the labour force because they want to or because they must? According to the Survey, one-quarter of all retired Canadians retired involuntarily, and a slightly higher proportion of men (27 per cent) than women (22 per cent) retired involuntarily.

The data suggest that among men, involuntary retirement is on the rise. Of men aged 45 to 59, 35 per cent retired involuntarily, compared to approximately 28 per cent of men in older age groups. However, the sample for the youngest age group is small and this finding must be treated cautiously. There is some evidence suggesting that women in younger age groups are less likely to retire involuntarily than their older counterparts.

Involuntary retirement varies across socio-economic status. It is more prevalent among workers from semi-skilled and unskilled occupations, among those with lower levels of education, and among those with lower incomes (see Appendix 5.3). This is the case for both men and women. Clearly, Canadians from the poorer end of the socio-economic spectrum are more likely to be placed unwillingly on a pathway to retirement.

But why do people retire if they would rather remain in the labour force? Chart 5.4 shows the reasons cited by voluntary and involuntary retirees. Two factors — health and mandatory retirement policies — are the primary reasons for involuntary retirement. The third most frequently cited reason is lack of work.

Table 5.4

Involuntary Retirement by Age Group and Sex
(per cent who retired involuntarily)

	All Ages	45-59	60-64	65-69	70-74	75-79	80 or over
All	25	23	25	27	22	26	24
Men	27	35*	28	28	23	28	26
Women	22	14*	19	27	21	24	21

*Estimate less reliable due to small sample size.

Source: Prepared by the Centre for International Statistics using Survey on Ageing and Independence microdata, 1991.

The Road to Retirement

Even among involuntary retirees, variations across socio-economic characteristics are evident. As shown in Chart 5.5, involuntary retirees from semi-skilled and unskilled occupations are more likely to have retired because of health problems and lack of work, and less likely to have retired because of mandatory retirement policies compared to retirees from "white-collar" occupations.

Evidence also suggests men are more likely than women to retire involuntarily because of health problems, mandatory retirement plans, and early retirement policies.

Involuntary retirement has important financial consequences. People retiring in this fashion are much more likely to have financial shortfalls in the adequacy of their household income. Twenty-three per cent indicate their household income is less than adequate in satisfying their current needs and 30 per cent expect their future household income to be less than adequate. Among voluntary retirees, only 10 per cent say their household income is less than

Chart 5.4

Reasons for Retirement Cited by Voluntary and Involuntary Retirees, Canada 1991

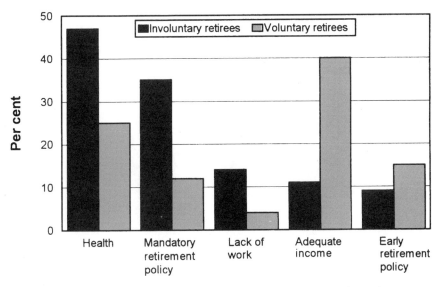

Source: Prepared by the Centre for International Statistics, using *Survey on Ageing and Independence* microdata, 1991.

adequate to satisfy their current needs and only 14 per cent expect this to be the case in the future. This difference may reflect the consequences of involuntary retirement, with people being forced out of the labour force before sufficient financial preparations have been made. It may also reflect the fact that the people most vulnerable to involuntary retirement, those with lower levels of education and in semi-skilled and unskilled jobs, are also likely to have relatively low earnings prior to retirement.

Overall, one in four Canadians enters retirement involuntarily, and this trend appears to be on the increase among men. People from unskilled and semi-skilled jobs, and those with lower levels of education and income are most likely to retire involuntarily. Health factors and mandatory retirement policies are the most prevalent reasons for doing so. Inadequacy of household income is associated with involuntary retirement.

Chart 5.5

Reasons for Retirement Among Involuntary Retirees by Occupation, Canada 1991

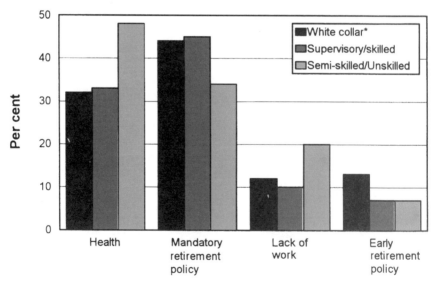

*Includes professional and semi-professional, senior and middle management, and technical occupations.

Source: Prepared by the Centre for International Statistics, using *Survey on Ageing and Independence* microdata, 1991.

A brief note on mandatory retirement

There has been considerable debate over mandatory retirement policies in recent years. Opponents argue that these policies should be prohibited because they discriminate on the basis of age and are a violation of human rights. Supporters argue that the benefits of mandatory retirement outweigh the restrictions imposed on individual rights, and that these restrictions, in accordance with the Canadian Charter of Rights and Freedoms, are within "...reasonable limits prescribed by law as can be demonstrably justified in a free and democratic society." The conventional arguments in support of mandatory retirement policies are that they promote work sharing, facilitate retirement planning among workers, facilitate work force planning among employers, minimize evaluation and monitoring of older workers on the job, and facilitate graduated pay scales that are not tightly linked to individual productivity.[15]

An important empirical question which often arises in this debate is: how many people would continue working if they were not forced out of the labour force by mandatory retirement? In 1991, approximately 320,000 retirees (of all ages) indicated that mandatory retirement policies were influential in their retirement decision. However, about half of these people said they retired voluntarily — that is, even though mandatory retirement policies were a consideration, they did not force the individual out of the labour force before he or she was ready. On the other hand, about 157,000 retirees said they would have preferred to continue working, but were forced to leave the labour force.

Some researchers have suggested that the financial consequences of mandatory retirement may not be too adverse, since the workers most affected "...tend to have higher wages and pensions and a long-term employment relationship, often with the protection of a formal collective agreement or personnel policy."[16] Estimates from the Survey on Ageing and Independence indicate that 74 per cent of retirees citing mandatory retirement policies have an employer-pension plan. This is the case for 79 per cent of men and 62 per cent of women. Of the people forced into retirement by mandatory retirement policies, three-quarters have employer-pension plans. This is the case for about 81 per cent of men and 63 per cent of women. Claims that people facing mandatory retirement policies are likely to have an employer-pension are valid to some extent, but many, particularly women, are excluded. And even among employees with coverage, those with low earnings or sporadic employment are likely to have limited pension entitlements. Preventing these individual from participating in paid employment is likely to impose severe financial hardship.

Relatively large proportions of people forced out of paid employment by mandatory retirement report they have inadequate income. One in five report that their household income is less than adequate to meet their current needs, and almost one in three expect their future income to be less than adequate.

Conclusions

Many of the conclusions drawn in earlier chapters have been reinforced in this analysis. There are many "pathways" to retirement and people enter into them for very different reasons. The movement of people into these pathways reflects the diversity and inequality in Canadian society. Women often retire for different reasons than men, and Canadians of lower socio-economic status retire for different reasons than those of higher socio-economic status.

The prevalence of involuntary retirement suggests that many people do not exercise control over the timing and nature of this transition. For many, forced retirement before the age of public pension eligibility (age 60 for partial CPP/QPP benefits and 65 for full benefits) is a reality. Increasing the age for public pension eligibility would have disastrous consequences for these individuals, since many already indicate their household incomes are less than adequate in meeting their needs.

Data indicating an increase in the rate of involuntary retirement is troubling. This form of retirement is most prevalent among the people who are least likely to afford premature retirement — those from semi- and unskilled occupations and with low levels of education. Continuation in this direction would no doubt increase income inequality among retired Canadians and generate greater dependence on public transfers to stave off poverty. As noted in Chapter Four, retirees with high levels of education and previous employment in professional and managerial occupations are most likely to return to the paid labour force after their initial retirement. Involuntary retirees generally do not have these characteristics and are less likely (or less able) to return to paid employment. Again, inadequacy of income and dependence on public transfers are likely outcomes.

CHAPTER 6 The Financing of Retirement

With Canadians leaving their jobs earlier and living longer, they are spending an increasing number of years outside of the labour force. How do they make ends meet during this stage of their lives? What sources of income do they rely upon? For a growing number of early retirees these questions are particularly pressing. As we have noted already, retirement and old age are no longer synonymous, and many people are leave the labour force well before they are eligible for a public pension or for other "old age" security benefits.

Questions about retirement income are also pertinent for a growing number of women making the transition out of the paid labour force. Their employment experiences differ significantly from those of men in terms of wages, unionization, hours of work, pension coverage and a host of other factors. What impact do these differences have on the financing of retirement? Do women rely on different sources of income than men?

The number of people opting to take partial CPP/QPP benefits before age 65 has skyrocketed.

The financing of retirement has come to the forefront of public attention in recent years for a number of reasons. The growth of government budget deficits and public debt has raised concern about the affordability of social programs, including Old Age Security (OAS) and the Canada/Quebec Pension Plans (CPP/QPP). These concerns have been exacerbated by the aging of the population and the growing proportion of non-employed Canadians relative to those employed. The promotion and popularity of RRSP have raised the question of whether Canadians are increasingly relying upon personal savings, as opposed to government transfers or employer-pension plans, as their primary source of retirement income.

By examining the retirement preparations made by Canadians and their sources of retirement income, we can begin to address these issues.

Financial Preparations for Retirement

Because the transition to retirement generally involves the loss of earnings from paid employment, most Canadians undertake financial preparations before retiring. Accumulating a financial reserve towards this end can be done in a number of ways, including building up savings in a bank account, investing in stocks, bonds or other assets, and contributing to a tax-assisted program such as an RRSP or a Registered Retirement Income Fund. One might also prepare by paying off (or avoiding) debts, or by making a major purchase — an automobile or household appliance, say — something which will be needed during one's retirement years, but is more sensibly bought while one still has an employment income.

In the Survey on Ageing and Independence, questions regarding financial preparations refer to those undertaken by the *household* in which the respondent lives. For example, did household members build up their savings, contribute to an RRSP or make other investments?

Retired Canadians

Foremost among household financial preparations for retirement is building up savings, done by 64 per cent of retirees. Paying off or avoiding debt follows close on the list, reported by 60 per cent of retirees, while almost half (47 per cent) contributed to an RRSP (see Table 6.1). Two less common forms of household financial preparation are making other (non-RRSP) investments (28 per cent) and making a major purchase (18 per cent) before retirement.

Table 6.1 shows that building up savings and paying off or avoiding debts are common forms of household preparation among retirees in all age categories. The prevalence of RRSP contributors declines with age. Part of this variation may be explained by the fact that RRSP legislation was passed in 1957 and was not a savings option, nor heavily promoted, during the working lives of many Canadians in

Table 6.1

Financial Retirement Preparations* Made by Retired Canadians, by Age Group, 1991 (per cent making preparations)

	Contribute to RRSP	Build up Savings	Make other Investments	Make Major Purchase	Pay Off/ Avoid Debt
All	47	64	28	18	60
45 to 59	63	54	29	20	58
60 to 64	64	69	33	16	60
65 to 74	52	65	28	20	61
75 & over	23	63	24	15	58

*Financial preparations refer to those made by the household in which the respondent lives.

Source: Prepared by the Centre for International Statistics using Survey on Ageing and Independence microdata,1991.

the older age groups. But this does not explain all the difference since Canadians who were aged 64, 69 and 74 at the time of the Survey on Ageing and Independence (1991) were aged 30, 35 and 40 at the time RRSP legislation was introduced. So the RRSP savings option was open to these individuals during much of their working lives.

The larger proportions of younger Canadians in households contributing to RRSPs may reflect the growing promotion and popularity of this program in recent years, plus the fear that government pension programs may be further cut back or eliminated. Also, RRSP contributions are based on earnings from employment, and since more women are participating in the labour force than in years past, an increasing number are now eligible to participate in the program. Finally, Table 6.1 does not take into account the age at which these individuals retired. By definition, those included in the youngest age categories retired early. Such early retirees may be more likely to actively prepare for retirement than those retiring at an older age, and may also be more likely to have relatively high incomes — a factor associated with RRSP contributions. Table 6.2 compensates for this factor by including only retirees who left the labour force before age 65. Again, the trend towards greater RRSP contributions among younger retirees is evident.

Household income is a key to retirement preparations. The Survey on Ageing and Independence provides data on respondents' household income in 1990, which for most reflects levels of pre-retirement income. As shown in Chart 6.1, there is a strong and consistent pattern between income and preparations of all types.

Table 6.2

Canadians Who Retired Before Age 65: Financial Retirement Preparations* by Age of Respondent (per cent)

Retirees Who Retired Before Age 65

	Contribute to RRSP	Make other Investments	Build up Savings	Pay-Off/ Avoid Debt	Make Major Purchases
60 to 64	65	34	69	60	16
65 to 69	60	32	69	61	21
70 to 74	41	26	65	65	20
75 & over	18	26	63	53	17

* Financial preparations refer to those made by the household in which the respondent lives.

Source: Prepared by the Centre for International Statistics using Survey on Ageing and Independence microdata, 1991.

Canadians still in the labour force

Many of the retirement preparations made by retirees are also being made by people still in the labour force. Paying off or avoiding debts, contributing to an RRSP and building up savings are the three most common forms of household financial preparations. As shown in Chart 6.2, there is, again, a positive and consistent relationship between household income and the likelihood of making household financial preparations for retirement. As income increases, people are considerably more likely to build up their savings, pay-off or avoid debt, contribute to an RRSP, make other (non-RRSP) investments or make a major purchase.

Earlier the higher proportion of retired Canadians in younger age groups contributing to RRSPs was noted. This suggests an emerging trend, which is confirmed by comparing the financial preparations made by Canadians already retired to those expecting to retire. As shown in Chart 6.3, the proportions of working Canadians contributing to an RRSP, making other investments and, to a lesser degree, pay-

Chart 6.1

Financial Retirement Preparations Made by Retired Canadians, by Household Income, 1991

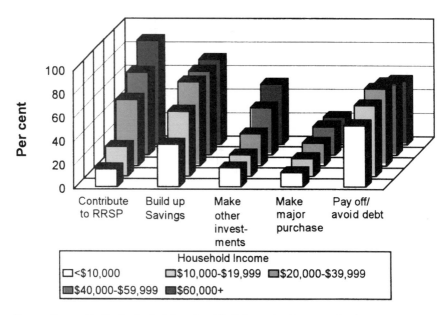

Source: Prepared by the Centre for International Statistics, using *Survey on Ageing and Independence* microdata, 1991.

ing off or avoiding debt exceed those of retired Canadians. Again, this suggests that working Canadians may be better financially prepared for retirement than were Canadians who already made this transition.

Other research also indicates that retirement preparations, particularly RRSP contributions, are becoming more popular. Hubert Frenken at Statistics Canada, for example, reports that RRSP contributions among women (aged 18 to 70) rose from 6 to 19 per cent between 1979 and 1989.[1] However, there remains a great range in the ability of people to make such preparations.

When employed respondents in the Survey were asked whether their income and investments would be adequate to enable them to retire as planned, 61 per cent said they would be adequate, 23 said they wouldn't and 16 per cent didn't know. Women are somewhat more likely than men to have concerns about the adequacy of their future retirement income. Not surprisingly, Canadians in higher income brackets and in managerial/professional occupations are much more likely to expect to have enough income to retire at the age they anticipate.

Chart 6.2

Financial Retirement Preparations Made by Employed Canadians, by Household Income, 1991

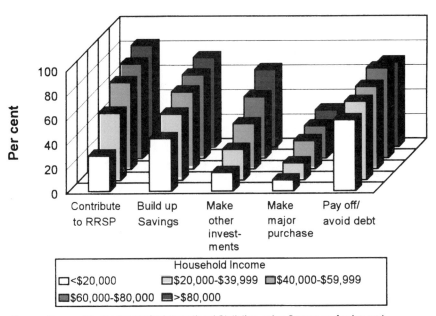

Source: Prepared by the Centre for International Statistics, using *Survey on Ageing and Independence* microdata, 1991.

Chart 6.3

Financial Retirement Preparations Made by Retired and Employed Canadians, 1991

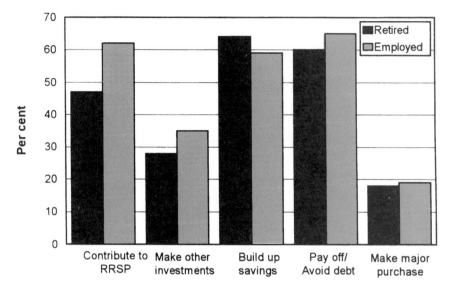

Source: Prepared by the Centre for International Statistics, using *Survey on Ageing and Independence* microdata, 1991.

Public and "Semi-private" Retirement Income

In examining the financing of retirement, it is useful to consider the broad structure of the income-security system for the elderly in Canada. This system is comprised of three components.[2] The first consists of public programs which provide a basic level of income to older Canadians. These include the Old Age Security pension (OAS), the Guaranteed Income Supplement (GIS), the Spouse's Allowance (SPA), and several provincial and territorial "top-up" programs. Income from these programs is not conditional on past contributions. The OAS is provided to all Canadian residents aged 65 and over, while the others are targeted towards older persons with low incomes.

The second component consists of the publicly administered Canada/Quebec Pension Plans (CPP/QPP). These programs "...are financed by contributions from workers and employers rather than from federal or provincial treasuries"[3] and individual benefits are based on past contributions.

"Semi-private" programs, including Registered Pension Plans (RPPs) and Registered Retirement Savings Plans (RRSPs), comprise the third component of income security for the elderly. These are privately organized and administered, and are generally viewed as falling outside of the realm of government.[4] They are only "semi-private," however, since they are subsidized by massive tax concessions on contributions and on earnings which accrue inside of the plans. In 1989, tax concessions on RRSPs totalled $4.2 billion and tax concessions on RPPs totalled $7.7 billion.[5] In other words, if the government had not provided tax breaks on RRSP and RPP contributions and earnings, it would have collected an additional $11.9 billion in revenue.

The sources of income received by retired Canadians reflects this dual system of public and semi-private income. Some retirees receive income only from public programs, such as OAS, GIS and CPP/QPP, while others also receive income from the semi-private sources of employer-pensions and RRSPs. This duality reflects divisions in the labour market.[6] Workers employed in the public sector and in large private sector manufacturing and financial institutions tend to receive private as well as public pensions.

> Those who must get by on the public system...tend to be in the "secondary" labor market made up of retail and consumer services, part-time employees, and small, labor-intensive firms. In view of sex differences in patterns of labor-force participation and occupational mix, the principal victims of this dualistic structure are also the fastest-growing sector of the labor market — women.[7]

This duality can be illustrated using data from the Survey on Ageing and Independence. Among employed persons aged 45 and over, 53 per cent of men and 42 per cent of women are covered by employer-pension plans.

As Table 6.3 shows, pension coverage is most prevalent among men and women in professional and managerial occupations, and least prevalent among those in semi-skilled and unskilled occupations. It is worth noting that, through the post-war period, men in semi-skilled and unskilled jobs have been concentrated in goods-producing industries where they have benefitted from high wages, extensive benefits and high rates of unionization. Women have been predominantly excluded from these industries, and instead, the semi-skilled and unskilled jobs filled by them have been in the service industries, characterized by low wages, few benefits and low rates of unionization.[8] This pattern of employment accounts, at least in part, for the relatively large difference in pension coverage between men and women in semi-skilled and unskilled occupations.

In terms of industries, pension coverage is most prevalent in public administration, distributive services (communications, utilities and transportation), community services (health, education and so on) and primary and manufacturing industries. At the other end of the spectrum, employees in agriculture, business and personal services, trade and construction are least likely to be included under an employer-pension.

Table 6.3

Employed Canadians Aged 45 and Over: Employer-Pension Plans by Sex and Selected Characteristics, Canada 1991 (per cent)

	All	Men	Women
	49	53	42
Occupation			
Professional & Senior Mgmt.	69	66	75
Semi-Prof./Technical/Mid-Mgmt.	58	62	54
Supervisory/Skilled	43	46	38
Semi-Skilled/Unskilled	43	52	31
Education			
Less than high school	38	45	29
High school graduate	49	54	43
Post-secondary graduate	58	61	54
Personal Income			
Less than $20,000	21	19	22
$20,000 to $39,999	60	57	64
$40,000 to $59,999	78	76	88
$60,000 or more	65	67	( )
Industry			
Public Administration	83	86	76
Community Services	67	78	61
Distributive Services	66	70	48
Primary & Manufacturing	59	65	39
Construction	39	41	( )
Finance	39	34	43
Trade	33	36	30
Business & Personal Services	26	31	21
Agriculture	9	9	10
Labour Force Status			
Working Full-time	56	57	54
Working Part-time	25	31	23

( ) Sample size too small to provide reliable estimate.

Source Prepared by the Centre for International Statistics using Survey on Ageing and Independence microdata, 1991.

The Road to Retirement

These findings are consistent with those reported elsewhere.[9] As Table 6.3 shows, pension coverage is also much less prevalent among part-time compared to full-time workers, accounting for part of the disparity in coverage between men and women. Published data also show that pension coverage is more prevalent among workers in larger firms, among unionized workers, and among workers employed in the public sector.[10]

Finally, as Table 6.3 shows, employer-pension coverage is more prevalent among workers in higher income categories. For example, while 19 per cent of men with personal incomes below $20,000 have pension coverage, this is the case for 67 per cent of those with incomes above $60,000. The pattern is similar among women.

Among retired Canadians, 62 per cent of men and 41 per cent of women receive income from an employer-pension plan. Pension cov-

Table 6.4

Average Income from Private and Public Pensions, by Age Group and Sex, Canada 1991

Average Annual Income from Pensions and Superannuations* other than CPP/QPP

	Men	Women	Women's Pension Income as a Percent of Men's
	($)	($)	
60 to 64	16,492	8,604	52%
65 to 69	11,345	6,034	53%
70 to 74	10,530	6,351	60%
75 & over	8,252	6,047	73%

Average Monthly Income from Canada Pension Plan**

	Men	Women	Women's Pension Income as a Percent of Men's
	($)	($)	
60 to 64	428	238	56%
65 to 69	510	287	56%
70 to 74	534	306	57%
75 to 79	445	273	61%
80 to 84	381	248	65%
85 & over	238	160	67%

* Estimates include Survivor Benefits paid upon death of original pension beneficiary.
** Estimates are for the month of June. Estimates do not include Survivor Benefits.

Source: Revenue Canada, *Taxation Statistics*, 1993 Table 4. Human Resources
      Development Canada ,*Canada Pension Plan - Old Age Security Statistical Bulletin*
      June 1994

erage among retirees varies across occupation, industry and income as it does among the employed population (see Appendix 6.1).

While access to employer-pensions is a key factor in retirement income, it is not the whole story. Even among those with pension coverage, benefit levels diverge considerably. As shown in Table 6.4, women between the ages of 60 and 69 receive about half the pension income received by men. This is because pension benefits are usually based on contributions made by workers as well as by employers. Because women are more likely than men to be employed on a part-time basis, to have lower earnings, and to experience employment disruptions because of family responsibilities, their pension contributions and subsequent benefits are lower. The same situation prevails in the public pension system. As shown in the lower half of Table 6.4, monthly CPP benefits received by women are only 55 to 65 per cent of those received by men.

Registered Retirement Savings Plans are also an important part of the semi-private system of retirement income in Canada. As noted earlier, RRSP contributions have become increasingly popular in recent years, and are most likely to be made by people in households with higher incomes. Table 6.5 emphasizes the latter point, showing the proportion of tax filers in different income groups who claimed an RRSP deduction on their personal income tax, the average deduction they claimed, and the average tax saving they received.

Table 6.5
RRSP Deductions by Income Category, Canada 1991

	RRSP Claimants as % of Taxfilers	Average Amount per Claimant	Average Tax Saving per Claimant
		($)	($)
All	24.2	2,896	1,135
$1 - $10,000	2.9	883	84
$10,000 - $20,000	14.2	1,429	358
$20,000 - $30,000	28.9	1,921	517
$30,000 - $40,000	42.2	2,458	1,017
$40,000 - $50,000	51.6	2,953	1,223
$50,000 - $60,000	58.0	3,503	1,452
$60,000 - $70,000	63.2	4,206	1,744
$70,000 - $80,000	67.3	5,092	2,352
$80,000 - $90,000	68.4	5,908	2,726
$90,000 - $100,000	71.7	6,592	3,040
$100,000 - $150,000	70.3	7,805	3,592
$150,000 +	73.1	10,342	4,769

Source: Prepared by the Centre for International Statistics using Revenue Canada, *Taxation Statistics*, 1993.

Clearly, people in higher income brackets are better able to contribute to an RRSP; moreover, because contributions are treated as tax deductions rather than as tax credits, they provide a larger tax saving to people in higher income brackets.[11] Overall, there are tremendous differences in the abilities of Canadians to access employer-pensions and RRSPs — the two key components of the semi-private system of retirement income. Those who do not benefit from these programs must rely on government pensions (CPP/QPP) and other public programs for their livelihood. The relative importance of these sources among retirees is evident in the Survey on Ageing and Independence.

In the Survey, respondents were asked to specify which source of their personal income they considered their main one. Retired women of all ages are much less likely than men to rely on private pensions as their main income source, and rely instead on government programs (including CPP/QPP, Old Age Security, Guaranteed Income Supplement and Spouse's Allowance). Indeed, fully 70 per cent of retired women aged 65 and over indicate that income from government programs are their financial mainstay (see Table 6.6). (Note, these estimates refer to retirees as defined in Chapter Two, not to the entire population of seniors, many of whom are not retired by our definition.)

Among both men and women, older retirees are less likely to rely on employer-pensions as their main source and more likely to rely on government pensions. For example, while 56 per cent of retired men

Table 6.6
Retired Canadians: Main Source of Personal Income by Age Group and Sex , Canada 1991

	Government Programs*	Employer Pensions	Investments	Other Sources**	Total
Men - All	41	41	12	7	100%
45 to 64	11	56	16	17	100%
65 to 74	46	39	10	5	100%
75 & over	57	31	11	1	100%
Women - All	58	22	13	7	100%
45 to 64	24	37	22	17	100%
65 to 74	70	18	10	2	100%
75 & over	72	18	8	2	100%

* Includes CPP/QPP, Old Age Security, Guranteed Income Supplement and Spouse's Allowance.
** Includes income from other government sources (including Unemployment Insurance, Social Assistance, Worker's Compensation, Disability Insurance, Family Allowance, and Veteran's Allowance) work, other family members,alimony, family inheritance and persons with no income.

Source: Prepared by the Centre for International Statistics using Survey on Ageing and Independence microdata, 1991.

aged 45 to 64 rely on private pensions, only 31 per cent of those aged 75 and over do so.

A number of factors contribute to this. First, many retirees in older age groups probably have had shorter periods of employer-pension contributions than those in younger age groups. Employer-pensions expanded through the 1960s. For a 45-year-old worker entering an employer-pension plan at that time, only 15 to 20 years would have been left during which to make contributions before retiring. For a 30-year-old worker, 30 years or more would have been left for making contributions. The importance of private pension income across different age cohorts likely reflects this difference.

Second, Canadians have experienced the erosion of their employer-pension benefits by inflation. For older retirees, pension entitlements which were adequate at the time of retirement (perhaps 10 or 15 years ago) are likely to be less than adequate after a decade or more of inflation. The employer-pension income of younger (more recently retired) Canadians has not been exposed to inflation for as long a period and, in some cases, has been indexed fully or partially to inflation. Moreover, while employer-pension plans earned high returns on invested funds during the 1966s as a result of high inflation, in many cases these returns did not accrue to older retirees. Instead, they were often used "to increase the size of unit benefits for active as opposed to retired plan members, or to lower employer contributions to pension plans." [12]

Third, retirees in younger age groups are more likely to have bene-fitted from improvements in pension portability, vesting, drop-out provisions and spousal benefits than their older counterparts. Many of these improvements have been implemented since the early 1980s and no doubt contribute to making employer-pensions a more viable, important and flexible source of retirement income for some retirees. However, these changes did little to improve the economic security of people excluded from employer-pensions, and reinforced, rather than lessened, the dualistic character of Canada's old age security system.

And finally, evidence from Australia indicates that persons retiring early on private income, such as pensions, superannuations, savings and other private sources, often become dependent on government transfers in later years. [13] This may reflect the exhaustion of private income sources and subsequent reliance on public sources.

Considerable differences also are evident when occupation, income and education are taken into account. As shown in Chart 6.4, there is a marked decline in reliance on employer-pension income among men as

Chart 6.4

Retired Men: Main Sources of Retirement Income by Occupation, Canada, 1991

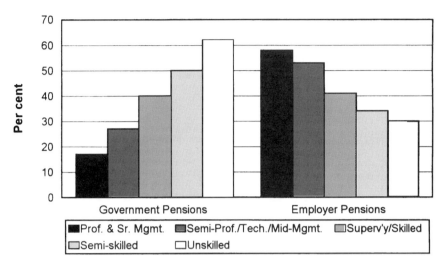

Source: Prepared by the Centre for International Statistics, using *Survey on Ageing and Independence* microdata, 1991.

Chart 6.5

Retired Women: Main Sources of Retirement Income by Occupation, Canada 1991

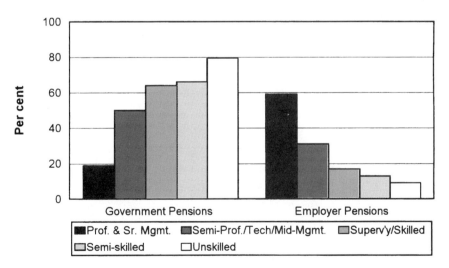

Source: Prepared by the Centre for International Statistics, using *Survey on Ageing and Independence* microdata, 1991.

Table 6.7

Retired Canadians Aged 45 and Over: Main Source of Income by Total Personal Income, Canada, 1991

	Government Programs**	Employer Pensions	Investments	Other Sources**	Total
Less than $10,000	73	6	9*	13	100%
$10,000 - $19,999	64	23	7	7	100%
$20,000 - $29,999	28	56	11	5*	100%
$30,000 - $39,999	10	67	19	3*	100%
$40,000 +	6*	61	27	6*	100%

* Estimate less reliable due to small sample size
** See note in Table 6.6 for definitions.

Source: Prepared by the Centre for International Statistics using Survey on Ageing and Independence microdata, 1991.

we look from professional and managerial to semi-skilled and unskilled occupations. Among women this pattern is not as noticeable, with over 60 per cent of women from all occupations (with the exception of professional and senior management positions) relying on government pensions as their main source of income (see Chart 6.5).

In terms of personal income, retirees in lower income groups are much more likely to rely on government pensions, and much less likely to rely on employer-pensions, than those in higher income groups (see Table 6.7). A similar pattern is evident between people with different levels of education.

Who gets the biggest piece of the pie?

So far, much has been said about the sources of retirement income, but little about its distribution. Is pension income held by relatively few retirees or is it widely dispersed among many?

To begin to address the question, male retirees have been categorized into income quintiles as shown in Table 6.8.[14] To produce these estimates, male retirees were ranked from lowest to highest on the basis of total personal income. They were then divided into five groups of equal size (quintiles). From this point, it is possible to ask how much of the total income reported by male retirees was received by those in the first, or poorest quintile, by those in the fifth, or richest quintile, and by those in-between.

As shown in Table 6.8, men in the poorest quintile receive about 10 per cent of total aggregate income. Those in the richest quintile receive about 40 per cent. This is the case among men aged 65 to 74 and men aged 75 and over. There is considerable variation in the distribution of

The Road to Retirement

Table 6.8

Distribution of Total Aggregate Income Across Income Quintiles, Canada 1991

Retired Men Age 65 to 74							
Income Quintile	Total Income	Private Income	Pensions & Superannuations*	Investments	Public Income	OAS, GIS SPA**	CPP/QPP
First (Poorest)	9	1	-	2	18	24	12
Second	13	4	3	5	21	23	20
Third	16	11	10	13	21	19	22
Fourth	23	25	25	23	21	18	23
Fifth (Richest)	39	59	62	57	19	16	23
Total	100%	100%	100%	100%	100%	100%	100%

Retired Men Age 75 & Over							
Income Quintile	Total Income	Private Income	Pensions & Superannuations	Investments	Public Income	OAS, GIS SPA	CPP/QPP
First (Poorest)	10	1	1	2	19	25	11
Second	13	4	3	4	22	23	20
Third	15	10	9	10	21	19	22
Fourth	21	23	21	24	19	17	20
Fifth (Richest)	42	62	66	60	20	16	27
Total	100%	100%	100%	100%	100%	100%	100%

*Also includes annuities. **Old Age Security, Guaranteed Annual Income Supplement and Spouse's Allowance

Source: Prepared by the Centre for International Statistics using Survey of Consumer Finances microdata, 1991.

income across quintiles when income from different sources are considered. Retired men in the richest quintile receive about 60 per cent of total aggregate income from private sources, including employer-pensions, investments, earnings and other private sources, while retired men in the poorest quintile receive about one to two per cent. A similar distribution is evident when pension and investment income are examined. Income from government transfers is more evenly distributed. Retirees in each income quintile receive approximately 20 per cent of total aggregate income from government transfers (public income). Those in the poorer quintiles receive larger shares of the income from Old Age Security, the Guaranteed Income Supplement and social assistance, while those in the richer quintiles receive larger shares of the income from the Canada/Quebec Pension Plans.

Overall, the wealthiest 20 per cent of retirees get the lion's share of income from private sources. This inequality is offset to some degree by government transfers, which are more evenly distributed among retirees.

This has changed little in the past decade. Comparing income distributions in 1981 and 1991 shows that the proportion received by retirees in each quintile vary by only a percentage point or two. The only difference of note is the decline in investment income received by men in the top quintile, explained by the fact that interest rates were exceptionally high in 1981, but had dropped to more typical levels in 1991.

The Financing of Early Retirement

With the trend towards early retirement, a increasing gap has emerged between the age at which people leave paid employment and the age at which they are eligible for a public pension. As noted in Chapter Three, nearly two-thirds of Canadians retire before age 65, the age at which they are eligible for a full public pension (CPP/QPP) and for OAS. One-third retire before age 60, when they are eligible for a partial CPP/QPP pension. How do these people finance their retirement when, for a relatively extended period, they have neither earnings from employment nor income from a public pension?

The data presented earlier in Table 6.6 provide some answers. The largest shares of men and, to a lesser degree, women who retire before age 65 say that employer-pensions are their main source of income. Smaller shares rely on investments, public old age security programs (CPP/QPP, OAS, GIS and SPA) and other government programs (including Unemployment Insurance, Worker's Compensation and social assistance). This overview can be expanded upon by examining a number of other data sources, including *Taxation Statistics*, the Survey of Consumer Finances, and administrative records from the Canada/Quebec Pension Plans. This closer investigation is warranted, given the increasing prevalence of early retirement.

Employer-pension plans

The importance of employer-pensions and superannuations in early retirement is confirmed when Revenue Canada's *Taxation Statistics* are reviewed. As shown in Table 6.9, the proportion of taxfilers aged 55 to 59 and 60 to 64 reporting income from pensions and superannuations increased through the 1980s. This increase is particularly striking among men, with almost a 100 per cent increase between 1981 and 1991.

Table 6.9

Taxfilers Receiving Income from Employer-Pensions and Other Superannuations by Age and Sex, Canada selected years (per cent)

	1981	1985	1991
Men			
55 to 59	8.3	11.5	15.5
60 to 64	19.8	27.9	34.4
Women			
55 to 59	7.4	7.4	10.3
60 to 64	18.5	19.4	23.1

Source: Prepared by the Centre for International Statistics using Revenue Canada's, *Taxation Statistics*, selected years.

The importance of employer-pensions is confirmed by evidence from the Survey of Consumer Finances (SCF). Table 6.10 includes retired men in the 55 to 59 and 60 to 64 age groups. The proportion of total aggregate income derived from specific sources are shown for these groups. That is, of *all* the income reported by all retired men, how much comes from employer-pensions, from investments and so on? Comparable data for women are not available.[15]

Among retired men aged 55 to 59, 80 per cent of total aggregate income is derived from private sources. The largest share of this income is from pensions and superannuations, with income from investments, earnings and other private sources accounting for much smaller shares. Public sources account for 20 per cent of the total aggregate income of retired men in this age group.

Overall, employer-pensions play an important role in the financing of early retirement. This attests to the use of early pension eligibility as one strategy used by businesses to alter the size and composition of their work forces. Many workers are being offered, and are opting to take, pension benefits before the "normal" age of 65. For workers who are ready to retire, these benefits provide a welcome opportunity to leave the labour force. For those who are not quite ready, early pension eligibility and severance packages may be a mixed blessing since they are often one-time offers. The older worker who opts to remain on the job rather than take a retirement package may face less generous arrangements or even layoff in the future. In this context, workers may "choose" to leave their jobs before they ready rather than risk retiring under poorer circumstances. In either case, employers exercise considerable power in the retirement transition, since the decision to offer early pension benefits or generous severance packages resides largely with them.[16]

Table 6.10

Retired Men: Sources of Total Aggregate Income by Age Group, Canada 1991

	Age 55 - 59	Age 60 - 64
Private Sources	80%	71%
earnings	2	2
pensions	62	53
investments	10	12
other private	5	4
Public Sources	20%	29%
CPP/QPP	11	20
OAS, GIS & SPA	0	1
other government	9	8
Total	100%	100%

Source: Prepared by the Centre for International Statistics using Survey of Consumer Finances microdata, 1991.

Canada/Quebec Pension Plans

Private funding has not been the only factor prompting retirement at younger ages. The Canada/Quebec Pension Plans have also played a role. In 1987, the Canada Pension Plan (CPP) was revised, allowing Canadians aged 60 to 64 to draw benefits at a reduced rate. Similar legislation was introduced in Quebec in 1984. As shown in Chart 6.6, the proportion of Canadians eligible for, and opting for, reduced CPP/QPP benefits at an earlier age increased from 20.3 per cent in 1987 to 37.6 per cent in 1993 — an increase of 85 per cent. And the increase has been equally striking among men and women.

There is a financial cost associated with taking pension benefits before age 65. The reduction rate is one-half of one per cent for every month before a person's 65th birthday. "In other words, people retiring 60 months early at the age of 60 lose 30 per cent of their normal CPP or QPP pension. The reduced rates are permanent and continue even after the pensioners turn 65." [17] For retirees with large incomes from private sources, this loss may not be too consequential. But for persons without adequate private income, particularly those forced into early retirement by unemployment, health problems or other factors, the reduction may result in financial hardship throughout their "golden years."

Chart 6.6

Proportion of Canadians Age 60 to 64 Receiving CPP/QPP Retirement Pensions, 1987-1993

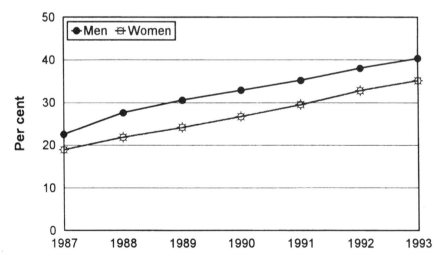

Source: Prepared by the Centre for International Statistics, using *Canada Pension Plan Statistical Bulletin* and *Le Regime de Rentes du Quebec*.

Disability pensions

Other income sources also appear to be important in the trend toward early retirement. In Canada, as in most other Western nations, there has been a marked increase in the number of disability pension recipients though the 1980s. Between 1980 and 1993 the number of Canadian men aged 55 to 64 receiving a disability pension through the Canada/ Quebec Pension Plans more than doubled, rising from 55,000 to 115,000. The number of female beneficiaries more than tripled over this period, rising from 20,000 to 61,000. This increase has been particularly striking since 1990, with over 17,000 new female beneficiaries joining the program in a three-year period. The number of applicants for disability pension under the CPP/QPP program has also been soaring.[18]

This increase does not simply reflect the growing number of people in this age group. Table 6.11 shows benefit recipients as a proportion of the total population aged 55 to 64. The number of male recipients increased from 5.6 to 9.9 per cent of the total population, while female recipients increased from 1.8 to 5.1 per cent. Expressed as a proportion of the employed labour force aged 55 to 64, the increase is even more striking.

Given the extreme magnitude of these increases, it seems unlikely that they reflect increases in the morbidity rate among older Canadians. Alternatively, because eligibility for disability benefits is based, in part, on prior contributions to the Canada/Quebec Pension Plans, the increase may reflect the rising labour force participation rate of older women and an increase in the proportion who are eligible for the program. However, this probably doesn't account for the rise among men, since no increase in eligibility (based on labour force participation rates) is evident.

Another explanation is that disability pensions are being used by displaced older workers to bridge the gap financially from the time they leave the labour force to the time they become eligible for a public pension. The use of disability pensions, as well as unemployment compensation, for this purpose has been documented in several European countries, including the Netherlands, West Germany, Sweden and Great Britain.[19] In these countries, older workers who are unable to find employment and are ineligible for public pensions are turning to disability pensions for financial support. In several countries, eligibility criteria for these pensions have been loosened to provide older workers with such support. Applicants are now

Table 6.11

Beneficiaries of CPP/QPP Disability Benefits
Aged 55 - 64, Canada 1980-1993

As Percent of Population Aged 55 - 64*

	1980	1985	1990	1993
Men	5.6	7.9	9.4	9.9
Women	1.8	2.8	3.7	5.1

As Percent of Labour Force Aged 55 - 64*

	1980	1985	1990	1993
Men	7.3	11.3	14.5	16.3
Women	5.5	8.4	10.4	14.0

Source: Calculations by author using, *Canada Pension Plan/Old Age Securtiy Statistical Bulletin*, *Le Régime de Rentes du Quebéc and Labour Force Annual Averages*, selected years.

screened on the basis of labour market characteristics as well as their own medical condition. For example, in the former West Germany, partially disabled persons might have received full benefits if there were no suitable part-time jobs, and in Sweden "jobless persons at least 60 years old may claim disability benefits until normal retirement at 65 if they cannot find employment."[20] In this sense, disability is being redefined on the basis of economic as well as health criteria.

In Canada, it remains to be seen whether disability pensions are being used as financial bridges to retirement. However, the dramatic rise in recipients (and applicants) for such pensions suggests this may well be the case. It raises a number of policy questions. Are additional public transfers and new programs needed to provide income support for older workers who are displaced from the labour market but are too young to qualify for public retirement pensions? Does the disability pension program have adequate resources to handle the growing number of applicants and recipients? Is the disability program now being called upon to meet a need that it was neither intended nor designed to meet? Further research into these issues is urgently required.

Social assistance

Given the trends in disability pensions, one question that arises regarding social assistance (welfare) is: Are some older workers being *forced* to use such programs as a financial bridge to retire-

Table 6.12

Proportion of Canadians Receiving Social Assistance by Age Group, Canada 1981 - 1991

	1981	1991	Percentage Point Change
15 to 24	3.0	4.9	(+) 1.9
25 to 44	3.5	6.7	(+) 3.2
45 to 54	3.9	5.1	(+) 1.2
55 to 59	5.6	7.5	(+) 1.9
60 to 64	7.6	9.1	(+) 1.5

Source: Prepared by the Centre for International Statistics using Survey of Consumer Finances microdata, 1982 and 1992.

ment? This is not inconceivable given the high rates and long durations of unemployment among older workers. One might speculate that those who use up their UI benefits and who are too young to qualify for Old Age Security are forced on welfare to make ends meet. As shown in Table 6.12, there has been an increase in the proportion of Canadians aged 55 to 64 receiving social assistance. However, similar increases are also evident among younger age groups, suggesting that economic pressures are forcing increasing numbers of Canadians of all ages to rely on government transfers rather than market earnings to get by.

Financing Retirement in the Future

With the aging of the population and the trend towards early retirement, a great deal of concern has arisen over the long-term financial viability of Canada's social programs. Specifically, will young workers be able to finance the pension and health care programs needed to sustain a growing number of elderly, non-working Canadians?

Two factors underlie this concern. First, with an older population, expenditures on public programs, especially health care and pensions, can be expected to increase. Ivan Fellegi, Chief Statistician of Canada, projects the average annual increase in expenditures on health care, pension and education programs will be as much as 2.3 per cent between 1986 and 2036.[21] Note that this is a compound rate of growth, and at this rate, the cost of these programs will double in about 31 years — by the year 2017. Projections by other analysts also "...support the general view that the increasing proportion of the elderly has the potential to increase public-sector costs substantially."[22]

The second factor causing concern is that there will likely be fewer people in the labour force to support these cost increases. Statistics Canada estimates that in 1986 there were 130 people outside the labour force for every 100 people in it — a ratio of 1.3 (known as the labour force dependency ratio). Projections of future labour force dependency ratios are based on assumptions of fertility and labour force participation rates. If labour force participation rates remain at 1986 levels, the dependency ratio is expected to rise from 1.3 to 1.6 or 1.7 by the year 2036.[23] That means there will be 160 to 170 Canadians outside the labour force for every 100 people in it. Alternatively, if labour force participation rates increase over the next 40 years as some forecasts show, the dependency ratio is expected to rise from 1.3 in 1986 to approximately 1.4 by the year 2036 — a more modest increase of approximately 10 per cent.[24]

Together, these factors have raised concerns that an unsupportable economic burden is being placed on young workers.

Will the financial viability of our social programs be undermined? Canada's chief statistician thinks they will not. Instead, he contends, rising expenditures will be offset by economic growth, provided that this growth continues to rise at the same annual rate that it has over the past 30 years.[25] Brian Murphy and Michael Wolfson, two researchers at Statistics Canada, reach a similar conclusion. They argue: "Contrary to many of the popularly expressed concerns, demographic aging is not the most important factor in determining future public-sector costs and revenues. Rather, aspects of the design and management of public-sector programs represent the greatest area of uncertainty."[26]

These researchers are not trying to diminish the importance of rising public sector expenditures. Rather, they are pointing out that other factors are as important as, and perhaps more so than, demographics in determining long-term public expenditures. This is good news. As Murphy and Wolfson point out, these latter factors, unlike demographic trends, "...are much more amenable to public policy."[27]

The question is, then: what types of public policies should be implemented? This opens up a myriad of issues and debates: reform of the Canada/Quebec Pension Plans, changes to RRSP legislation, reform of employer-pension plans, changes to the Old Age Security program, and so on. It is well beyond the scope of this chapter to delve into these issues, each of which warrants detailed assessment.

Suffice to say, the broad conceptual framework of this chapter — the dualistic structure of semi-private and public sources of retirement income — provides a useful analytical tool for assessing policy directions. Policies may be interpreted as pushing Canada's system of retirement income towards one side or the other of this dichotomy.

Ellen Gee and Susan McDaniel, two Canadian sociologists, argue that "the overall thrust of pension politics in recent years has been towards privatization."[28] In 1989, a "claw-back" provision was introduced into the OAS program, so that people with annual incomes of $50,000 or more must pay back some or all of their OAS benefit. While this may not appear to be cause for concern, the claw-back is not fully indexed to inflation. "Therefore, the number of older persons subject to the claw-back will increase each year," and it is estimated that under the current proposal, people retiring in the year 2019 with as little income as $20,000 (in 1989 dollars) will have their OAS benefits reduced.[29]

At the same time that this public program has been eroded, however, semi-private programs have been strengthened. The rules governing RRSPs have been changed recently, with the maximum amount people are allowed to contribute substantially increased. This is an indication that greater responsibility for retirement income is being placed on individuals rather than government. But as shown earlier (Table 6.5), the ability of individuals to participate in the RRSP program varies dramatically by income, and the tax benefits fall disproportionately to the rich. Similarly, improvements have been made to the employer-pension system, and while benefitting members, these changes have done nothing to improve the financial security of people who are excluded.

Conclusions

The diversity in retirement apparent in earlier chapters is evident in this one as well. Men and women, and people with different socioeconomic characteristics, rely on different sources of retirement income. Registered Retirement Savings Plans and employer-pensions constitute a semi-private system of retirement income which remains inaccessible to many Canadians — mainly women and older people. Instead, these retirees rely more on government programs (CPP/QPP, Old Age Security, the Guaranteed Income Supplement and Spouse's Allowance) as their main sources of retirement income. Policies that erode these programs will decrease the financial security of many people and reinforce income inequalities among Canada's older population. It would be tragic to turn back the clock and eliminate the gains made in the fight against poverty among the elderly.

In terms of early retirement, employer-pensions play an important role. Many early retirees report that these pensions are their main source of income. This fact, coupled with the increasing use of financial incentives to encourage older workers to leave their jobs, shows that employers are now using retirement as a way to cut-back and reorganize their work forces. For many workers, this is a welcome development. For others, the situation of "retire now or take your chances" is a mixed blessing at best.

Public programs also have played an important role in the trend towards early retirement. The number of people opting to take partial CPP/QPP benefits before age 65 has been skyrocketing. For some, this is a welcome opportunity to leave the labour force. But for others, such as the long-term unemployed, it is one of the few alternatives open to them. Early CPP/QPP benefits may also encourage employers to target older workers for layoffs, since these workers have alternative sources of income available to them.[30]

The extraordinary increase in the number of older workers receiving disability pensions is a cause for concern. This increase may be symptomatic of the lack of financial alternatives for older workers facing involuntary retirement at relatively young ages. This raises the question of whether additional public transfers and new programs are needed to provide income support for early retirees who do not have adequate private income, and whether older unemployed workers need better access to retraining and re-employment programs.

CHAPTER 7 What's Down the Road?

This has been a book about change and diversity—change in how and when people retire and diversity in the characteristics of retirees themselves. Both have increased throughout the 1980s and 1990s. But what of the future? What will retirement be like for Canadians a decade or two from now? Obviously, we can't answer these questions with certainty, but we can speculate about a few key issues.

Is early retirement becoming a permanent feature of the Canadian labour market, or is it just a phase we are going through? A look at changing labour market conditions over the past 30 years is instructive. In the 1970s, the size of the labour force grew rapidly at an average annual rate of 3.2 per cent, with the number of workers increasing from 8.6 million in 1971 to 11.9 million in 1981.[1] This was largely a result of the baby boom generation coming of working age (15 years and over) as well as the dramatic increase in the number of women entering paid employment. Throughout the 1980s, however, growth was much slower. In that decade, fewer young Canadians (the "baby-bust" generation) entered the labour force, and female labour force participation rates grew at a slower rate. Consequently, between 1981 and 1991, the annual growth of the labour force averaged only 1.5 per cent — less than half of that witnessed during the previous decade.[2] And this decline is expected to continue, putting the growth rates for the 1990s below one per cent.

With fewer and fewer younger workers entering the labour force and more and more older workers leaving it, a major labour shortage may be looming in the not-too-distant future. If this happens, employers may look to older workers as a source of labour, encouraging them to stay on the job by offering them financial incentives and more flexible work arrangements. Government, too, might try to encourage older workers to remain in the labour force by restricting access to public pensions. In this scenario, the current trend towards early retirement could be quickly turned around.

On the other hand, with the introduction of new technology and the reorganization and streamlining of business operations, the anticipated demand for labour may be less than expected. Firms may replace some workers with machines or move some operations, such as product assembly, to countries where labour costs are low.

Moreover, even if labour were in short supply, the demand for it might be met by encouraging more women to enter the labour force or by changing immigration policies. The employment prospects of older workers may not improve.

At the same time, any deliberate attempts to reverse the trend towards early retirement — to offset real or anticipated labour shortages — would be hampered by popular expectations. Most Canadians expect to leave the labour force before age 65, and changes in public policies inhibiting them from doing so would likely meet with public opposition. The OECD cautions that if early retirement schemes, such as eligibility for partial CPP/QPP benefits at age 60, "... are instituted in response to a short-term problem, such as a rise in unemployment, it becomes difficult to limit them to...one particular group of older workers. Expectations of early retirement can then become institution-alised."[3] That being the case, any government efforts to change such schemes at a later date would no doubt be very difficult.

Strains and conflicts between younger and older generations are a possibility in the coming years, given the economic pressures associated with an aging population and growing numbers of retired people. The public pension system is a potential troublespot. Between 1966 and 1986, the contribution rate to the CPP/QPP was 3.6 per cent, shared equally between employees and employers. That is, employees contributed 1.8 per cent of their eligible earnings to the program and employers matched this. In 1987 the rate was increased for the first time, to 3.8 per cent. It has been increased by 0.2 per cent in each subsequent year (to 5.2 per cent in 1994), and will continue to rise to offset payments to an increasing number of beneficiaries. By the year 2010, the CPP contribution rate is projected to reach 8.9 per cent, and by 2025, 12.4 per cent — more than triple the rate between 1966 and 1986.[4] This, coupled with cost increases in other areas, such as public health care, could increase dissatisfaction among some younger workers who feel they are subsidizing an aging population. Consequently, debates about the direction of public pro-grams and government spending, which have long been argued from different regional and ideological perspectives, may also be argued from the viewpoint of age.

There have been some improvements in the labour market experi-ences of women in the past 10 to 15 years. Although the majority of women remain in "traditional" occupations, such as clerical, sales and service jobs, a growing proportion are entering other occupations, such as managerial, professional and administrative positions.[5] For example, in 1982 women accounted for 18 per cent of all doctors, dentists and other health professionals (excluding nursing and related occupations); by 1991 this had risen to 27 per cent. Women have also been acquiring higher levels of education. In 1975, they received 44 per cent of all bachelor's degrees granted by Canadian universities; in 1990 they received 56 per cent of such degrees.[6] The proportion of women in previously male-dominated areas, such as commerce, medicine and law, also has risen substantially.

All this bodes well for the future. As shown throughout this book, labour market characteristics are influential in shaping all aspects of the retirement transition. As the labour market position of women improves, so too will their retirement options.

However, there are still fundamental inequalities between the sexes. Women employed on a full-time, full-year basis still earn only about 70 per cent as much as their male counterparts.[7] And, women are more likely than men to be employed part-time and to experience career disruptions because of their responsibilities for domestic labour and child care. Consequently, the retirement options open to them will continue to be limited by their disadvantaged position within the labour market.

One can visualize older workers along a continuum. At one end are those who are not able to exercise much control over their retirement; at the other are those who have a great deal of control. The former may include workers facing retirement due to job termination or long-term unemployment. They receive little or no compensation for losing their jobs, and because of obsolete skills, lack of union protection, health problems or other factors, they have few options in the labour market. These workers retire not on their own terms, but on terms forced on them.

A little further across the spectrum are workers who have some control over the way that they will retire. This group may include workers who are offered employer-pension benefits at an early age, on the condition that they leave their jobs. Some may choose to keep on working but they risk layoff in the future under less favourable circumstances. Others may choose to take their pension and either retire or look for another job, depending on their financial resources. These workers are able to make decisions about their retirement, but only within a range of options dictated to them.

And finally, at the other end of the spectrum are workers who exercise considerable control over their retirement. These people face little or no pressure to leave their jobs, and are able to time their retirement to maximize their financial security. This is most possible for those with high salaries, private investments and pension entitlements. When and how they retire is for them to decide.

Older workers are located all along this continuum. Whether their position shifts towards one end or the other in the coming years remains to be seen. If unemployment rates remain high and employers continue to target older workers for layoffs, a growing number will be unable to exercise much choice in their retirement decisions. Their range of options would be narrowed further if the government, prompted by concern over the debt, increased the eligibility age for full or partial CPP/QPP benefits, or limited access to other supports such as Unemployment Insurance. On the other hand, labour market opportunities and control over retirement would be enhanced if greater emphasis were placed on the retraining and re-employment of older workers. Likewise, flexible work arrangements making partial retirement a more viable employment option would offer a compromise between full-time employment and complete withdrawal from the labour market. Such arrangements would also provide employers with an alternative to the early retirement incentives and layoffs traditionally used to reorganize their work forces.

These scenarios are not necessarily mutually exclusive. Control over retirement may well improve for some Canadians while deteriorating for others. In recent years, the concept of "polarization" has been central in many important labour market studies. The former Economic Council of Canada documents a growing cleavage between "good jobs" and "bad jobs."[8] Good jobs are those with high wages, good benefits, high skill requirements and employment security; bad jobs are those lacking these traits. Increasingly, employed Canadians are clustered at one pole or the other, with fewer and fewer in the middle.[9] In the coming decades, the retirement prospects for people who have spent a lifetime in "bad jobs" will no doubt pale beside those available to people in "good jobs." In this context, the diversity already evident in the retirement transition could become much more extreme.

Appendix

Appendix 3.1

Labour Force Participation Rates for Men and Women Age 65 & over, Canada 1946 - 1993

	Men	Women
1946	47.5	5.0
1947	44.9	5.7
1949	42.9	4.7
1951	37.9	4.1
1953	34.8	3.6
1955	32.3	3.9
1957	34.1	5.0
1959	31.0	5.2
1961	29.3	5.9
1963	26.4	5.9
1965	26.3	6.0
1967	24.7	5.9
1969	23.5	5.5
1971	20.0	5.1
1973	18.1	4.4
1975	18.5	4.9
1977	15.6	4.4
1979	15.3	4.2
1981	14.1	4.5
1983	13.1	4.2
1985	12.4	4.3
1987	11.9	3.6
1989	11.1	3.5
1991	11.3	3.5
1993	10.2	3.7

Source: Statistics Canada, *Labour Force Annual Averages, 1975-1983;
Labour Force Annual Averages, 1981-1988*; *Annual Averages,
1991, 1993*; Lynn McDonald and Mervin Chen, "*The Youth Freeze
and the Retirement Bulge.*" *Journal of Canadian Studies, Vol.28,
No.1, 1993.*

Appendix 3.2

Retired Canadians: Age of Retirement by Selected Characteristics, Canada 1991

	Actual Age of Retirement				
	Age 59 or Younger	Age 60 to 64	Age 65	Age 66 or Older	Total
All	32	32	25	12	100%
Men	27	32	28	12	100%
Women	38	31	20	11	100%
Occupation - Men					
Professional/Managerial	28	31	21	20	100%
Semi-Prof./Technical/Mid-Mgmt.	35	33	23	9	100%
Supervisory/Skilled	29	31	25	15	100%
Semi-skilled/Unskilled	17	35	38	10	100%
Occupation - Women					
Professional/Managerial	44	33	17	7	100%
Semi-Prof./Technical/Mid-Mgmt.	35	37	18	10	100%
Supervisory/Skilled	36	28	23	13	100%
Semi-skilled/Unskilled	36	31	21	13	100%
Education - Men					
Less than high school	22	34	33	12	100%
High school graduate	35	30	23	11	100%
Post-secondary graduate	33	32	21	14	100%
Education - Women					
Less than high school	32	32	23	13	100%
High school graduate	46	26	20	8	100%
Post-secondary graduate	41	34	15	10	100%
Employer-Pensions - Men					
Has pension	29	35	28	7	100%
Does not have pension	24	28	27	21	100%
Employer-Pensions - Women					
Has pension	32	37	24	7	100%
Does not have pension	43	27	17	14	100%
Sector - Men					
Private sector	25	34	28	13	100%
Public sector	32	33	29	6	100%
Sector - Women					
Private sector	39	30	19	12	100%
Public sector	36	34	24	7	100%

Source: Prepared by the Centre for International Statistics using Survey on Ageing and Independence microdata, 1991.

Appendix 3.3

Retired Canadians: Age of Retirement by Selected Characteristics, Canada 1991

Actual Age of Retirement

	Age 59 or Younger	Age 60 to 64	Age 65	Age 66 or Older	Total
Industry - Men					
Agriculture & Other Primary	29	28	22	22	100%
Manufacturing	22	36	32	11	100%
Construction	15	30	35	20	100%
Transport/Communication/Utilities	26	38	31	5	100%
Wholesale/Retail Trade	26	30	29	15	100%
FIRE*/Business & Personal Serv.	24	32	30	14	100%
Community services	20	28	29	24	100%
Public Administration	34	33	29	5	100%
Industry - Women					
Agriculture & Other Primary	33	35	15	17	100%
Manufacturing	41	37	18	5	100%
Construction	( )	( )	( )	( )	( )
Transport/Communication/Utilities	( )	( )	( )	( )	( )
Wholesale/Retail Trade	36	25	26	13	100%
FIRE*/Business & Personal Serv.	31	35	22	13	100%
Community services	45	27	14	13	100%
Public Administration	36	34	25	5	100%
Class of Worker - Men					
Paid employee	27	34	29	10	100%
Self-employed	29	25	22	24	100%
Class of Worker - Women					
Paid employee	38	31	21	10	100%
Self-employed	44	29	10	17	100%
Personal Income - Men					
Less than $10,000	31	23	30	16	100%
$10,000 to $19,999	21	32	34	13	100%
$20,000 to $39,999	27	37	26	10	100%
$40,000 or more	43	28	18	11	100%
Personal Income - Women					
Less than $10,000	50	22	18	9	100%
$10,000 to $19,999	29	36	21	13	100%
$20,000 to $39,999	33	37	22	9	100%
$40,000 or more	( )	( )	( )	( )	( )

FIRE includes Finance, Insurance and Real Estate. () Sample size too small to provide reliable estimate.

Source: Prepared by the Centre for International Statistics using Survey on Ageing and Independence microdata, 1991.

The Road to Retirement

Retired Canadians: Age of Retirement by Selected Household Characteristics, Canada 1991

Actual Age of Retirement

	Age 59 or Younger	Age 60 to 64	Age 65	Age 66 or Older	Total
Marital Status - Men					
Married/Common-Law	28	33	28	11	100%
Not Married	25	31	28	16	100%
Marital Status - Women					
Married/Common-Law	50	30	15	6	100%
Not Married	28	32	24	16	100%
Household Income - Men					
Less than $10,000	31	18	35	17	100%
$10,000 to $19,999	21	33	32	13	100%
$20,000 to $39,999	25	35	29	11	100%
$40,000 to $59,999	34	36	21	9	100%
$60,000 or more	55	20	15	10	100%
Household Income - Women					
Less than $10,000	41	18	24	17	100%
$10,000 to $19,999	25	36	25	14	100%
$20,000 to $39,999	37	35	17	10	100%
$40,000 to $59,999	62	26	9	4	100%
$60,000 or more*	56	32	9	4	100%

* Estimate less reliable due to small sample size.

Source: Prepared by the Centre for International Statistics using Survey on Ageing and Independence microdata, 1991

Appendix 3.5

Retired Canadians: Age of Retirement by Selected Health Characteristics, Canada 1991

	Actual Age of Retirement				
	Age 59 or Younger	Age 60 to 64	Age 65	Age 66 or Older	Total
Health Status - Men					
Excellent	35	27	25	13	100%
Good	24	35	30	12	100%
Fair/Poor	27	34	27	12	100%
Health Status - Women					
Excellent	45	26	18	11	100%
Good	35	32	22	11	100%
Fair/Poor	39	33	17	12	100%
Comparative Health Status - Men					
Better	24	31	30	16	100%
Same	27	35	28	10	100%
Worse	45	25	22	9	100%
Comparative Health Status - Women					
Better	34	32	21	13	100%
Same	40	32	19	9	100%
Worse	55	20	14	11	100%
Presence of Physical Limitation - Men					
With limitation	32	31	27	10	100%
No limitations	25	33	28	13	100%
Presence of Physical Limitation - Women					
With limitation	40	28	20	11	100%
No limitations	37	32	19	11	100%

Source: Prepared by the Centre for International Statistics using Survey on Ageing and Independence microdata, 1991.

Appendix 3.6
Employed Canadians: Expected Age of Retirement by Selected Characteristics, Canada 1991

Expected Age of Retirement

	Age 59 or Younger	Age 60 to 64	Age 65	Age 66 or Older	Total
All	28	34	34	5	100%
Men	26	33	35	6	100%
Women	30	35	32	3	100%
Occupation - Men					
Professional/Managerial	32	32	32	5	100%
Semi-Prof./Technical/Mid-Mgmt.	38	30	28	4	100%
Supervisory/Skilled	23	39	33	5	100%
Semi-skilled/Unskilled	20	30	42	7	100%
Occupation - Women					
Professional/Managerial	53	28	15	5	100%
Semi-Prof./Technical/Mid-Mgmt.	26	36	35	2	100%
Supervisory/Skilled	31	39	26	4	100%
Semi-skilled/Unskilled	22	34	42	2	100%
Education - Men					
Less than high school	19	36	39	6	100%
High school graduate	28	34	31	7	100%
Post-secondary graduate	31	30	34	5	100%
Education - Women					
Less than high school	25	38	35	2	100%
High school graduate	27	35	35	2	100%
Post-secondary graduate	37	32	27	4	100%
Employer Pensions - Men					
Has pension	33	34	29	4	100%
Does not have pension	14	31	46	9	100%
Employer Pensions - Women					
Has pension	37	33	28	2	100%
Does not have pension	23	37	36	4	100%

( ) Sample size too small to provide reliable estimate.

Source: Prepared by the Centre for International Statistics using Survey on Ageing and Independence microdata, 1991.

Appendix 3.7

Employed Canadians: Expected Age of Retirement by Selected Characteristics, Canada 1991

Expected Age of Retirement

	Age 59 or Younger	Age 60 to 64	Age 65	Age 66 or Older	Total
Industry - Men					
Agriculture & Other Primary	15	32	43	11	100%
Manufacturing	24	37	37	2	100%
Construction	21	40	32	8	100%
Transport/Communication/Utilities	41	26	27	6	100%
Wholesale/Retail Trade	17	35	43	6	100%
FIRE*/Business & Personal Serv.	32	30	35	4	100%
Community Services	23	30	36	11	100%
Industry - Women					
Agriculture & Other Primary	16	39	37	8	100%
Manufacturing	35	31	31	2	100%
Construction	25	42	32	1	100%
Transport/Communication/Utilities	29	41	29	1	100%
Wholesale/Retail Trade	29	27	39	5	100%
FIRE*/Business & Personal Serv.	33	37	27	3	100%
Community Services	27	42	30	1	100%
Public Administration	36	22	38	4	100%
Job Tenure - Men					
Less than one year	17	37	38	9	100%
1 to 10 years	17	31	44	8	100%
11 to 20 years	25	38	33	4	100%
More than 20 years	38	32	26	5	100%
Job Tenure - Women					
Less than one year	22	47	28	3	100%
1 to 10 years	30	34	33	4	100%
11 to 20 years	35	32	31	2	100%
More than 20 years	38	34	24	3	100%
Weeks Worked Past Year - Men					
0 to 25	6	30	53	10	100%
26 to 48	13	40	41	7	100%
49 to 52	29	33	32	6	100%
Weeks Worked Past Year - Women					
0 to 25	18	37	44	1	100%
26 to 48	28	42	25	5	100%
49 to 52	33	33	31	3	100%

( ) Sample size too small to provide reliable estimate.

Source: Prepared by the Centre for International Statistics using Survey on Ageing and Independence microdata, 1991.

The Road to Retirement

Appendix 3.8

Employed Canadians: Expected Age of Retirement by Selected Household Characteristics, Canada 1991

Expected Age of Retirement

	Age 59 or Younger	Age 60 to 64	Age 65	Age 66 or Older	Total
Labour Force Status - Men					
Working full-time	28	34	34	5	100%
Working part-time	( )	( )	( )	( )	( )
Looking for work	11	30	55	4	100%
Labour Force Status - Women					
Working full-time	33	34	31	2	100%
Working part-time	26	37	32	5	100%
Looking for work	18	35	43	5	100%
Personal Income - Men					
Less than $10,000	( )	( )	( )	( )	( )
$10,000 to $19,999	14	25	56	5	100%
$20,000 to $39,999	20	34	40	6	100%
$40,000 to $59,999	38	36	23	3	100%
$60,000 or more	33	34	26	8	
Personal Income - Women					
Less than $10,000	20	30	47	3	100%
$10,000 to $19,999	26	41	30	3	100%
$20,000 to $39,999	32	36	29	3	100%
$40,000 to $59,999	46	33	18	3	100%
$60,000 or more	( )	( )	( )	( )	( )

( ) Sample size too small to provide reliable estimate.

Source: Prepared by the Centre for International Statistics using Survey on Ageing and Independence microdata, 1991

Appendix 3.9

Employed Canadians: Expected Age of Retirement by Selected Household Characteristics, Canada 1991

Expected Age of Retirement

	Age 59 or Younger	Age 60 to 64	Age 65	Age 66 or Older	Total
Marital Status - Men					
Married/Common-Law	25	34	35	5	100%
Not Married	30	27	35	8	100%
Marital Status - Women					
Married/Common-Law	35	35	27	2	100%
Not Married	17	34	44	4	100%
Labour Force Status of Spouse					
Male Respondents					
Working full-time	28	31	36	5	100%
Working part-time	29	37	27	8	100%
Unemployed/Not in labour force	20	38	37	4	100%
No spouse present	30	27	35	8	100%
Labour Force Status of Spouse					
Female Respondents					
Working full-time	40	33	25	2	100%
Working part-time	27	43	26	4	100%
Unemployed/Not in labour force	19	37	41	3	100%
No spouse present	17	34	44	4	100%
Household Income - Men					
Less than $20,000	7	25	64	5	100%
$20,000 to $39,999	19	35	41	6	100%
$40,000 to $59,999	31	34	31	5	100%
$60,000 to $80,000	28	41	28	3	100%
More than $80,000	39	33	22	6	100%
Household Income - Women					
Less than $20,000	10	30	55	5	100%
$20,000 to $39,999	22	34	41	3	100%
$40,000 to $59,999	37	32	28	3	100%
$60,000 to $80,000	41	42	15	3	100%
More than $80,000	56	34	10	0	100%

Source Prepared by the Centre for International Statistics using Survey on Ageing and Independence microdata,1991

Employed Canadians: Expected Age of Retirement by Selected Health Characteristics, Canada 1991

Expected Age of Retirement

	Age 59 or Younger	Age 60 to 64	Age 65	Age 66 or Older	Total
Health Status - Men					
Excellent	25	33	35	7	100%
Good	28	33	34	5	100%
Fair/Poor	22	34	40	5	100%
Health Status - Women					
Excellent	32	33	31	3	100%
Good	29	37	31	3	100%
Fair/Poor	27	33	37	3	100%
Comparative Health Status - Men					
Better	24	35	34	7	100%
Same	28	33	35	4	100%
Worse	29	23	43	5	100%
Comparative Health Status - Women					
Better	28	35	33	4	100%
Same	32	33	32	2	100%
Worse	31	42	22	5	100%
Presence of Physical Limitations - Men					
With limitation	28	31	34	7	100%
No limitations	26	33	36	6	100%
Presence of Physical Limitations - Women					
With limitation	29	33	32	6	100%
No limitations	31	35	32	2	100%

Source Prepared by the Centre for International Statistics using Survey on Ageing and Independence microdata, 1991.

Non-Standard Employment by Age and Sex, Canada 1989

	Total Employment (000s)	Percent Non-Standard *	Percent Non-Standard **
All	12,468	**22**	**31**
Men	6,933	**16**	**25**
15 to 24	1,151	41	45
25 to 34	2,057	13	21
35 to 44	1,805	8	19
45 to 54	1,183	8	22
55 to 64	736	16	25
Women	5,535	**31**	**37**
15 to 24	1,091	48	51
25 to 34	1,654	25	31
35 to 44	1,427	29	37
45 to 54	906	26	33
55 to 64	457	30	37

* Includes any of part-time work, part-year work or temporary work.

** Includes any of own-account self-employment, part-time work, part-year work, temporary work, and multiple job holding.

Source: Harvey Krahn, *"Non-standard work arrangements." Perspectives on Labour and Income* Ottawa: Statistics Canada, Cat.# 75-001, Vol.3 No.4 (Winter 1991): p.42.

Retired Canadians: Reasons for Retirement by Selected Characteristics, Canada 1991

	Wanted to Stop Working	Adequate Retirement Income	Health	Mandatory Retirement Policy
All	56	34	30	18
Men	54	38	32	21
Women	58	27	29	13
Occupation - Men				
Professional/Managerial	56	48	19	21
Semi-Prof./Technical/Mid-Mgmt.	61	55	22	18
Supervisory/Skilled	57	39	29	20
Semi-skilled/Unskilled	52	31	33	24
Occupation - Women				
Professional/Managerial	62	44	20	15
Semi-Prof./Technical/Mid-Mgmt.	60	31	20	17
Supervisory/Skilled	63	29	23	11
Semi-skilled/Unskilled	55	20	34	14
Education - Men				
Less than high school	51	31	36	21
High school graduate	55	46	27	20
Post-secondary graduate	58	46	25	21
Education - Women				
Less than high school	55	21	34	14
High school graduate	61	28	25	14
Post-secondary graduate	60	38	23	11
Personal Income - Men				
Less than $10,000	39	18	51	13
$10,000 to $19,999	48	26	37	21
$20,000 to $39,999	60	48	26	24
$40,000 or more	62	63	15	18
Personal Income - Women				
Less than $10,000	54	14	39	9
$10,000 to $19,999	55	28	27	16
$20,000 to $39,999	65	45	22	15
$40,000 or more	( )	( )	( )	( )

Appendix 5.1 (continued)

	Early Retirement Policy	Lack of Work	Provide Family Care
All	14	7	9
Men	18	6	5
Women	7	7	13
Occupation - Men			
Professional/Managerial	24	5	5
Semi-Prof./Technical/Mid-Mgmt.	23	5	6
Supervisory/Skilled	19	4	5
Semi-skilled/Unskilled	15	9	5
Occupation - Women			
Professional/Managerial	17	1	20
Semi-Prof./Technical/Mid-Mgmt.	8	6	10
Supervisory/Skilled	5	8	13
Semi-skilled/Unskilled	5	9	15
Education - Men			
Less than high school	12	7	5
High school graduate	27	4	5
Post-secondary graduate	25	7	5
Education - Women			
Less than high school	4	8	15
High school graduate	9	5	14
Post-secondary graduate	10	8	11
Personal Income - Men			
Less than $10,000	3	12	6
$10,000 to $19,999	10	9	6
$20,000 to $39,999	23	3	4
$40,000 or more	36	2	5
Personal Income - Women			
Less than $10,000	3	11	18
$10,000 to $19,999	10	6	12
$20,000 to $39,999	8	3	8
$40,000 or more	( )	( )	( )

( ) Sample size too small to provide reliable estimate.

Source: Prepared by the Centre for International Statistics using Survey on Ageing and Independence microdata, 1991

The Road to Retirement

Table 5.2

Persons Who Retired Before Age 65: Selected Reasons for Retirement by Sex and Current Age, Canada 1991 (per cent)

	Early Retirement Policies	Adequate Retirement Income	Health
Men			
60 to 64	39	46	36
65 to 69	22	38	39
70 to 74	23	48	38
75 & over	18*	39	39
Women			
60 to 64	()	32	36
65 to 69	()	29	39
70 to 74	()	29	29
75 & over	()	26	29

* Estimate less reliable due to small sample size.
() Sample size too small to provide reliable estimates.

Source: Prepared by the Centre for International Statistics using Survey on Ageing and Independence microdata, 1991.

Appendix 5.2 (continued)

	Early Retirement Policy	Lack of Work	Provide Family Care
All	19	18	8
Men	20	15	7
Women	17	22	9
Occupation - Men			
Professional/Managerial	24	9	5
Semi-Prof./Technical/Mid-Mgmt.	29	14	5
Supervisory/Skilled	16	12	4
Semi-skilled/Unskilled	20	22	9
Occupation - Women			
Professional/Managerial	27	15	8
Semi-Prof./Technical/Mid-Mgmt.	13	22	6
Supervisory/Skilled	19	19	11
Semi-skilled/Unskilled	14	29	9
Education - Men			
Less than high school	18	19	8
High school graduate	22	15	6
Post-secondary graduate	21	12	5
Education - Women			
Less than high school	12	25	11
High school graduate	22	21	10
Post-secondary graduate	18	20	7
Personal Income - Men			
Less than $20,000	10	28	8
$20,000 to $39,999	18	16	6
$40,000 to $59,999	32	11	7
$60,000 or more	24	11	8
Personal Income - Women			
Less than $20,000	11	25	11
$20,000 to $39,999	20	22	7
$40,000 to $59,999	26	12	3
$60,000 or more	( )	( )	( )

( ) Sample size too small to provide reliable estimate.

Source Prepared by the Centre for International Statistics using Survey on Ageing and Independence microdata, 1991.

Involuntary Retirees by Sex and Selected Characteristics, Canada 1991

	Percent retiring involuntarily		
	All	**Men**	**Women**
Occupation			
Professional/Managerial	15	16	14
Semi-Prof./Technical/Mid-Mgmt.	22	19	25
Supervisory/Skilled	21	23	19
Semi-skilled/Unskilled	28	30	25
Education			
Less than high school	28	30	25
High school graduate	21	24	17
Post-secondary graduate	22	24	20
Personal Income			
Less than $10,000	27	36	24
$10,000 to $19,999	31	35	24
$20,000 to $39,999	19	21	15
$40,000 or more	13	15	( )

( ) Sample size too small to provide reliable estimate.

Source: Prepared by the Centre for International Statistics using Survey on Ageing and Independence microdata, 1991.

Appendix 6.1

Retired Canadians Age 45 and Over: Percent With Employer-Pensions by Sex and Selected Characteristics, Canada 1991

	All	Men	Women
	53	**62**	**41**
Occupation			
Professional & Senior Mgmt.	74	76	71
Semi-Prof./Technical/Mid-Mgmt.	60	66	53
Supervisory/Skilled	53	63	39
Semi-Skilled/Unskilled	45	56	28
Education			
Less than high school	45	54	29
High school graduate	58	68	47
Post-secondary graduate	65	74	55
Industry			
Public Administration	83	85	77
Distributive Services	76	80	( )
Community Services	65	73	61
Primary & Manufacturing	64	71	41
Finance	49	( )	( )
Trade	37	48	28
Construction	31	34	( )
Business & Personal Services	23	37	( )
Agriculture	5	6	( )
Personal Income			
Less than $10,000	18	19	19
$10,000 to $19,999	49	52	45
$20,000 to $39,999	76	77	72
$40,000 or more	77	84	( )

( ) Sample size too small to provide reliable estimate.

Source Prepared by the Centre for International Statistics using Survey on Ageing and Independence microdata, 1991

The Road to Retirement

Appendix 6.2
Retired Canadians: Distribution Across Personal and Household Income by Sex and Age, Canada 1991

Personal Income

	Age 45 to 64			Age 65 & Over		
	All	Men	Women	All	Men	Women
Less than $10,000	29	9*	52	19	11	32
$10,000 - $19,999	26	31	21*	43	42	45
$20,000 - $39,999	28	37	18*	30	38	19
$40,000 or more	17	23	()	7	10	()
Total	100%	100%	100%	100%	100%	100%

Household Income

	Age 45 to 64			Age 65 & Over		
	All	Men	Women	All	Men	Women
Less than $20,000	23	26	19	46	39	56
$20,000 - $39,000	34	37	31	38	42	31
$40,000 - $59,000	22	18*	25*	10	13	()
$60,000 or more	21	19*	()	6	6	()
Total	100%	100%	100%	100%	100%	100%

* Estimate less reliable due to small sample size.
() Sample size too small to provide reliable estimate.

Source Prepared by the Centre for International Statistics using Survey on Ageing and Independence microdata, 1991

ENDNOTES

CHAPTER ONE

1 Bertrand Desjardins, *Population Ageing and the Elderly* (Ottawa: Statistics Canada, Cat. 91-533E), 1993.

2 Vanier Institute of the Family, *Profiling Canada's Families* (Ottawa: Vanier Institute of the Family, 1994), p. 74. Also see Maureen Moore, "Dual-Earner Families: The New Norm" in *Canadian Social Trends*, 12 (Spring, 1989), p. 25.

3 Forum Directors Group, "Keynote Paper," *Family Security in Insecure Times* (Ottawa: Canadian Council on Social Development, 1993), pp. 2-3.

4 These include Health and Welfare Canada, Veterans Affairs Canada, the Seniors Secretariat, Fitness and Amateur Sport, Consumer and Corporate Affairs, Canada Mortgage and Housing Corporation and the Department of the Secretary of State and Communications Canada. The survey was designed with the assistance of the Canadian Aging Research NETwork (CARNET).

5 "Residents of the Yukon and Northwest Territories, residents of institutions, persons living on Indian reserves and members of the Armed Forces were not included in the survey...." Readers should note that 8 per cent of Canadians aged 65 and older (and 24 per cent of Canadians aged 80 and older) live in institutions. This portion of the elderly population is not represented in the survey. Statistics Canada, The Survey on Ageing and Independence: Microdata User's Guide, (Ottawa: Statistics Canada, 1992), Appendix G.

6 This is adapted from Anne-Marie Guillemard, "International Perspectives on Early Withdrawal from the Labour Force." *States, Labor Markets, and the Future of Old-Age Policy*, edited by John Myles and Jill Quadagno (Philadelphia: Temple University Press, 1991), p. 209.

CHAPTER TWO

1 W. Kenneth Bryden, Old Age Pensions and Policy Making in Canada, (Doctoral dissertation, University of Toronto, 1970), p. 57.

2 John Myles, *Old Age in the Welfare State: The Political Economy of Pensions*, (University of Kansas Press, 1989), p. 7.

3 Ibid., p. 8.

4 William Graebner, *A History of Retirement: The Meaning and Function of An American Institution, 1885-1978* (New Haven: Yale University Press, 1980), p. 11.

5 Ibid. Also see Myles, p. 8.

6 Statistics Canada, *Historical Statistics of Canada*, edited by F.H. Leacy (Ottawa: Statistics Canada, Cat. CS11-516E, 1983), Series R812-825.

7 Bryden, p. 65, and Ellen Gee and Susan McDaniel, "Pension Politics and Challenges: Retirement Policy Implications," *Canadian Public Policy*, 17, 4 (1991), p. 465.

8 Frank Laczko and Chris Phillipson, *Changing Work and Retirement: Social Policy and the Older Worker* (Philadelphia: Open University Press, 1991), p. 13.

9 Ibid., pp. 13-14.

[10] See discussion in Myles, pp. 11-15, and in Frank Laczko and Chris Phillipson, pp. 13-15.

[11] Graebner, pp. 22-24.

[12] Industrial Relations Section, School of Commerce and Administration, Queen's University, *Industrial Relations Plans in Canada* (Kingston: Queen's University, 1938).

[13] Ibid., p. 5.

[14] Ibid.

[15] Quoted in Myles, p. 13.

[16] Bryden, p. 79.

[17] Chris Phillipson, *Capitalism and the Construction of Old Age* (London: The MacMillan Press Ltd. 1982), pp. 22-23.

[18] Myles, p. 14.

[19] Myles, p. 21.

[20] Bryden reports that in 1931 there were less than 10,000 inmates over age 60 in all charitable and benevolent institutions. In that year the population aged 70 and over alone numbered 345,000. Bryden, pp. 61-62.

[21] Ibid.

[22] Ibid., p. 66.

[23] Myles, p. 16.

[24] Ibid., p. 17.

[25] Health and Welfare Canada, *Social Security Statistics, Canada and the Provinces 1958-59 to 1982-83* (Ottawa: Minister of National Health and Welfare, September 1985), p. 59.

[26] Ibid, p. 61 and p. 73.

[27] Bryden, p. 65.

[28] Lynn McDonald and Mervin Chen, "The Youth Freeze and the Retirement Bulge: Older Workers and the Impending Labour Shortage," *Journal of Canadian Studies*, 28, 1 (Spring, 1993): p. 88.

[29] Martin Kohli and Martin Rein, "The changing balance of work and retirement," *Time for Retirement: Comparative Studies of Early Exit from the Labour Force*, edited by Martin Kohli et al. (Cambridge: Cambridge University Press, 1991), p. 6.

[30] Anne-Marie Guillemard, "International Perspectives on Early Withdrawal from the Labour Force," *States, Labor Markets, and the Future of Old-Age Policy*, Edited by John Myles and Jill Quadagno (Philadelphia: Temple University Press, 1991).

[31] Ibid., p. 212.

[32] Kohli and Rein, p. 5.

[33] Seniors Secretariat, *Ageing and Independence: Overview of a National Survey* (Ottawa: Minister of Supply and Services Canada, 1993. Cat. H88-3/13-1993), p. 34.

[34] Gary S. Fields and Olivia S. Mitchell, *Retirement, Pensions, and Social Security* (Cambridge: The MIT Press, 1984), p. 4.

35   Lea Achdut and Yossi Tamir, "Retirement and Well-being Among the Elderly." *Poverty, Inequality and Income Distribution in Comparative Perspective: The Luxembourg Income Study*, edited by Timothy Smeeding et al. (Washington, D.C.: The Urban Institute Press, 1990), pp. 105-125.

36   See Herbert Parnes, "The Retirement Decision," *The Older Worker* (Madison: Industrial Relations Research Association, 1988), p. 119.

CHAPTER THREE

1   Martin Kohli and Martin Rein, "The changing balance of work and retirement." *Time for Retirement: Comparative Studies of Early Exit from the Labour Force*, edited by Martin Kohli et al. (Cambridge: Cambridge University Press, 1991), p. 6.

2   Ibid.

3   Tom Schuller, "Work-Ending: Employment and Ambiguity in Later Life," *Becoming and Being Old: Sociological Approaches to Later Life*, edited by Bill Bytheway et al. (London: Sage Publications, 1989), p. 52.

4   See Anne-Marie Guillemard and Herman van Gunsteren, "Pathways and their prospects: A comparative interpretation of the meaning of early retirement." *Time for Retirement: Comparative Studies of Early Exit from the Labour Force*, edited by Martin Kohli et al. (Cambridge: Cambridge University Press, 1991), pp. 375-377.

5   Organisation for Economic Cooperation and Development, "Labour Market Participation and Retirement of Older Workers." *Employment Outlook*, July 1992 (Paris: OECD, 1992) pp. 201-202.

6   This estimate is calculated from Frank Denton and Sylvia Ostry, *Working-Life Tables for Canadian Males* (Ottawa, Dominion Bureau of Statistics, 1969), Table 1, p. 25. Estimates of participation rates from this source are slightly higher than those from the 1961 Census.

7   This includes people who are in the labour force (either employed or unemployed) as well as people who were not in the labour force at the time of the Survey, but who had been in it in the past and who planned on returning to it in the future.

8   David Ekerdt, Barbara Vinich and Raymond Bosse, "Orderly Endings: Do Men Know When They Will Retire?" *Journal of Gerontology*, 44, 1 (1989), p. S28.

9   Ibid.

10   Because of the institutional recognition of age 65 as a retirement benchmark, this has been defined as the "normal" retirement age. Only a small proportion of Canadians actually retired (12 per cent) or expect to retire (5 per cent) at age 66 or older. This has been defined as "late" retirement. Almost two-thirds of Canadians actually retired or expect to retire before the age of 65. While "early" retirement could be defined as age 64 and younger, this provides a relatively blunt measure. Grouping such a large proportion of the population into a single category is likely to conceal as many differences as are revealed. To facilitate a more sensitive analysis, two categories of "early" retirement have been defined, the first defined as age 59 and younger, the second defined as age 60 to 64.

[11]   O. Mitchell, P. Levine and S. Pozzebon, "Retirement Differences by Industry and Occupation," *The Gerontologist*, 28, 4 (1988) pp. 545-551

[12]   Gary S. Fields and Olivia S. Mitchell, *Retirement, Pensions and Social Security*, (Cambridge: The MIT Press, 1984), p. 546. M. Hayward, W. Grady, M. Hardy and D. Sommers (1989), "Occupational Influences on Retirement, Disability, and Death," *Demography*, 26, 3 (1989), pp. 393-409. Mark Hayward and William Grady, "Work and Retirement Among a Cohort of Older Men in the United States, 1966-1983," *Demography*, 27, 3 (1990), pp. 337-356.

[13]   For example, see: Rachel Floersheim Boaz, "Early Withdrawal from the Labor Force: A Response Only to Pension Pull or Also to Labor Market Push." *Research on Aging*, 9, 4, (1988) pp. 530-547. M. Hayward, D. Grady, W. Hardy and D. Sommers, pp. 393-409. Linda George, Gerda Fillenbaum and Erdman Palmore, "Sex Differences in the Antecedents and Consequences of Retirement," *Journal of Gerontology*, 39, 3 (1984), pp. 364-371.

[14]   Linda George, Gerda Fillenbaum and Erdman Palmore, pp. 364-371.

[15]   This pattern is reported elsewhere. See: Victor Fuchs, "Self-Employment and Labor Force Participation of Older Males," *Journal of Human Resources*, 17, 3 (1982), pp. 339-358. Mark Hayward and William Grady, pp. 337-356. Rachel Floersheim Boaz, pp. 530-547.

[16]   In the Survey on Ageing and Independence, information on labour force status, weeks worked and job tenure is available for those still in the labour force. Consequently, analysis of these variables is restricted to the expected age of retirement indicated by working Canadians.

[17]   Maureen Moore, "Dual-Earner Families: The New Norm," *Canadian Social Trends*, 12 (1989), p. 25.

[18]   In 1970 the average age for first marriage was 25.1 years for men and 22.7 years for women. By 1990 these figures were 27.9 and 26.0 years. Similarly, in 1971 the average age of mothers at the birth of their first child was 23.3; in 1990 it was 26.4. The Vanier Institute of the Family, *Profiling Canadian Families* (Ottawa: The Vanier Institute of the Family, 1994), pp. 39, 57.

[19]   See Hubert Frenken, "Marriage, money and retirement." *Perspectives on Labour and Income*, 3, 4 (Winter 1991), pp. 31-34.

[20]   Because the spouses of most retired respondents are also retired and data on their labour force histories are unavailable, this analysis is limited to employed respondents.

[21]   Herbert Parnes, "The Retirement Decision," *The Older Worker*, edited by Industrial Relations Research Association (Madison: Industrial Relations Research Association, 1988), p. 121.

[22]   See G. Bazzoli, "The early retirement decision: New empirical evidence on the influence of health," *Journal of Human Resources*, 20, 2 (1985), pp. 97-101. Robert Myers, "Why Do People Retire from Work Early," *Social Security Bulletin*, 45 (1982), pp. 10-14.

[23]   For diverse views see: G. Bazzoli op. cit.; also Thomas Chirikos and Gilbert Nestel, "Occupational Differences in the Ability of Men to Delay Retirement," *The Journal of Human Resources*, 17, 1 (1991), pp. 1-27.

[24] See: Tom Schuller, op. cit.; also Frank Laczko, "Between Work and Retirement: Becoming 'Old' in the 1980s," *Becoming and Being Old: Sociological Approaches to Later Life*, edited by Bill Bytheway et al. (London: Sage Publications, 1989), pp. 24-40.

[25] Anne-Marie Guillemard, "International Perspectives on Early Withdrawal from the Labour Force," *States, Labor Markets, and the Future of Old-Age Policy*, edited by John Myles and Jill Quadagno (Philadelphia: University Press, 1991), p. 224.

[26] Anne-Marie Guillemard and Herman Van Gunsteren, pp. 375-377.

[27] Ibid., p. 383.

[28] Linda George, Gerda Fillenbaum and Erdman Palmore, pp. 364-371.

CHAPTER FOUR

[1] Frank Laczko, Angela Dale, Sara Arber and G. Nigel Gilbert, "Early Retirement in a Period of High Unemployment," *Journal of Social Policy*, 17, 3 (1988), pp. 313-333. Organisation for Economic Cooperation and Development, "Labour Market Participation and Retirement of Older Workers," *Employment Outlook*, July 1992 (Paris: OECD, 1993), pp. 205-213.

[2] *Bridges to Retirement: Older Workers in a Changing Labor Market.* Edited by Peter Doeringer (Ithaca: ILR Press, Cornell University, 1990).

[3] Ibid., Chapter Five.

[4] Lynn McDonald and Mervin Chen, "The Youth Freeze and the Retirement Bulge: Older Workers and the Impending Labour Shortage," *Journal of Canadian Studies*, 28, 1 (Spring 1993), p. 85.

[5] *Time for Retirement: Comparative Studies of Early Exit from the Labour Force*, edited by Martin Kohli, Martin Rein, Anne-Marie Guillemard and Herman van Gunsteren (Cambridge: Cambridge University Press, 1991).

[6] Martin Kohli and Martin Rein, "The changing balance of work and retirement," *Time for Retirement* (endnote 5).

[7] Frank Laczko and Chris Phillipson, *Changing Work and Retirement: Social Policy and the Older Worker* (Philadelphia: Open University Press, 1991), p. 47.

[8] Calculations by author. Statistics Canada, *Historical Labour Force Statistics*, 1993 (Ottawa: Minister of Industry, Science and Technology, Cat 71-201, February 1994), p. 258.

[9] This is calculated by dividing the total number of persons aged 45 to 64 who are not in the labour force, but who looked for work in the previous 6 months, but did not look during the reference week because they believed no jobs were available, by the total number of persons aged 45 to 64 who are unemployed.

[10] Ernest Akyeampong, "Job Loss and Labour Market Adjustment." *The Labour Force* (November 1987), p. 107.

[11] Ibid.

[12] Jason Siroonian, "A note on the recession and early retirement," *Perspectives on Labour and Income*, 5, 4 (Winter 1993) p. 10.

13 Frank Laczko, "Between Work and Retirement: Becoming 'Old' in the 1980s." *Becoming and Being Old: Sociological Approaches to Later Life*, edited by Bill Bytheway et al. (London: Sage Publications, 1989), p. 27. See also: Frank Laczko et al., "Early Retirement in a Period of High Unemployment," pp. 313-333.

14 See Harvey Krahn, "Non-standard work arrangements," *Perspectives on Labour and Income*, 3, 4 (Winter, 1991), pp. 34-45.

15 Economic Council of Canada, *Good jobs, Bad jobs: Employment in the Service Economy* (Ottawa: Minister of Supply and Services Canada, 1991), p. 81.

16 Harvey Krahn, pp. 35-36.

17 Chris Foster, *Towards a National Retirement Incomes Policy*, Social Security Review, Australia, Issues Paper No. 6, 1988, p. 73. See also: P.L. MacDonald and R.A. Warner, "Part-time Work and the Older Worker in Canada," *Working Part-Time: Risks and Opportunities*, edited by B. Warme et al. (New York: Praeger, 1992).

18 Lars Osberg, "Is It Retirement or Unemployment? The Constrained Labour Supply of Older Canadians" (Statistics Canada, October, 1988).

19 Ernest B. Akyeampong, "Flexitime work arrangements," *Perspectives on Labour and Income*, 5, 3 (Autumn 1993), p. 17.

20 Economic Council of Canada, p. 13.

21 Grant Schellenberg, "Benefits for part-time workers," *Perception*, 18, 1 (1994), pp. 14-16.

22 Anne-Marie Guillemard and Herman van Gunsteren, "Pathways and their prospects: A comparative interpretation of the meaning of early retirement." *Time for Retirement: Comparative Studies of Early Exit from the Labour Force*, edited by Martin Kohli et al. (Cambridge: Cambridge University Press, 1991), pp. 369-370.

23 Joseph Tindale, *Older Workers in an Aging Work Force* (Ottawa: National Advisory Council on Aging, Cat. H71-2/1-10-1991E, 1991), pp. 42-43.

24 Ibid.

CHAPTER FIVE

1 Frank Laczko, "Between Work and Retirement: Becoming 'Old' in the 1980s," *Becoming and Being Old: Sociological Approaches to Later Life*, edited by Bill Bytheway et al. (London: Sage Publications, 1989), p. 27. See also: Frank Laczko, Angela Dale, Sara Arbers and G. Nigel Gilbert, "Early retirement in a period of high unemployment," *Journal of Social Policy*, 17, 2 (1988), pp. 313-34.

2 Frank Laczko, pp. 35-39.

3 Herbert Parnes, "The Retirement Decision," *The Older Worker*, edited by Industrial Relations Research Association (Madison: Industrial Relations Research Association), p. 121.

4 In 1991, 56 per cent of women were employed in just three occupations: clerical, sales and service jobs. Statistics Canada, *Labour Force Annual Averages*, 1991 (Ottawa: Minister of Industry, Science and Technology, Cat. 71-220, 1992), calculated from Table 15, p. B-41.

---

5 See Hubert Frenken and Karen Maser, "Employer-sponsored pension plans: who is covered?" *Perspectives on Labour and Income*, 4, 4 (Winter 1992), pp. 27-34.

6 Wallace Clement and John Myles, *Relations of Ruling: Class and Gender in Postindustrial Societies* (Montreal: McGill-Queen's University Press, 1994), pp. 175-181.

7 Statistics Canada, *The Daily*, Cat. 11-001 (April 13, 1993), calculated from Table on p. 8.

8 Diane Galarneau, "Women approaching retirement," *Perspectives on Labour and Income*, 3, 3 (Autumn, 1991), pp. 28-39.

9 Statistics Canada, *The Labour Force* (April, 1993), p. C8.

10 Clement and Myles, pp. 175-187.

11 Age 65, rather than age 60, was chosen as the cut-off for early retirement to maximize the number of respondents within the analysis. Defining early retirement as before age 60 results in small samples sizes within age cohorts, especially if men and women are examined separately.

12 OECD, "Labour Market Participation and Retirement of Older Workers." *Employment Outlook*, July 1992 (Paris: OECD, 1992), p. 196.

13 Galarneau, pp. 28-39.

14 David Ekerdt, Barbara Vinich and Raymond Bosse, "Orderly Endings: Do Men Know When They Will Retire?" *Journal of Gerontology*, 44, 1 (1989), p. S28.

15 Morley Gunderson and James Pesando, "The Case for Allowing Mandatory Retirement," *Canadian Public Policy*, 14, 1 (1988), pp. 32-39. For an overview of the argument against mandatory retirement see: Michael Krashinsky, "The Case for Eliminating Mandatory Retirement: Why Economics and Human Rights Need Not Conflict," *Canadian Public Policy*, 14, 1 (1988), pp. 40-51.

16 Morley Gunderson and James Pesando, p. 33.

CHAPTER SIX

1 Hubert Frenken, "Women and RRSPs," *Perspectives on Labour and Income*, 3, 4 (Winter 1991), pp. 8-13.

2 National Council of Welfare, *A Pension Primer* (Ottawa: Minister of Supply and Services Canada, Cat. H68-23/1989, 1989), pp. 1-2.

3 Ibid., p. 18.

4 John Myles and Les Teichroew, "The Politics of Dualism: Pension Policy in Canada," *States, Labor Markets, and the Future of Old-Age Policy*, edited by John Myles and Jill Quadagno (Philadelphia: Temple University Press, 1991), p. 91.

5 Department of Finance, *Government of Canada: Personal Income Expenditures* (Ottawa: Department of Finance, December 1992), p. 13.

6 Myles and Teichroew, pp. 91-92.

7 Ibid.

8 See Wallace Clement and John Myles, *Relations of Ruling: Class and Gender in Postindustrial Societies* (Montreal: McGill-Queens University Press, 1994), pp. 63-90.

⁹ Hubert Frenken and Karen Maser, "Employer-sponsored pension plans: who is covered?" *Perspectives on Labour and Income*, 4, 4 (Winter, 1992), pp. 27-34.

¹⁰ Ibid.

¹¹ See National Council of Welfare, *A Pension Primer* (Ottawa: Minister of Supply and Services, Cat. H68-23/1989E, September, 1989), pp. 49-50.

¹² Government of Canada, *Better Pensions for Canadians* (Ottawa: Minister of Supply and Services, Cat. 45-28/1982E, 1982), pp. 12-13.

¹³ Chris Foster, *Towards a National Retirement Incomes Policy* (Social Security Review, Australia, Issues Paper No. 6, 1988), p. 62.

¹⁴ In this analysis of the Survey of Consumer Finances (SCF), retirees are defined as respondents who receive income from a public or private pension, and whose income from wages, salaries and self-employment does not exceed 25 per cent of total personal income. This definition uses pension income as the main criterion, but recognizes that some retirees also earn a small share of their income from paid employment. This income-based definition is required because appropriate information is not available in the SCF to define retirees on the basis of subjective or labour market criteria.

However, not all people receiving income from the Canada/Quebec Pension Plans have previously been in the labour force. Some receive benefits as a result of pension splitting upon divorce or separation, or receive Survivor's Benefits following the death of a spouse who was a beneficiary. This results in an overestimation of the number of women defined as retired.

In June 1994, 91 per cent of the recipients of Survivor's Pensions aged 65 and over were women. Approximately half of these women (201,247) received *only* Survivor's Pensions. That is, they did not receive Retirement Pensions of their own because they had not previously participated in the paid labour force (or did not work enough hours to qualify). Only 3 per cent (1,304) of the men receiving Survivor's Pensions did not receive Retirement Pensions benefits as well. Because of the overestimation of retired women, financial information is unreliable. Consequently, the analysis is presented for men only.

¹⁵ See endnote 14.

¹⁶ Anne-Marie Guillemard, "International Perspectives on Early Withdrawal from the Labor Force," *States, Labor Markets, and the Future of Old-Age Policy*, edited by John Myles and Jill Quadagno (Philadelphia: Temple University Press, 1991), p. 222.

¹⁷ National Council of Welfare, p. 20.

¹⁸ This information was confirmed in a telephone conversation with Wayne Ganim, Acting Director of the Canada Pension Plan.

¹⁹ Guillemard, pp. 218-223.

²⁰ Anne-Marie Guillemard and Herman von Gunsteren, "Pathways and their prospects: A comparative interpretation of the meaning of early exit." *Time for Retirement: Comparative Studies of Early Exit from the Labour Force*, edited by Martin Kohli et al. (Cambridge: Cambridge University Press, 1991), p. 376.

21 Ivan Fellegi, "Can We Afford an Aging Society," *Canadian Economic Observer* (October, 1988), pp. 4.1 - 4.34.

22 Brian Murphy and Michael Wolfson, "When the Baby Boom Grows Old: Impacts on Canada's Public Sector," Statistics Canada, Analytical Studies Branch, Paper No. 38, 1991, p. 19.

23 Michael Wolfson, "International Perspectives on the Economics of Aging," *Canadian Economic Observer* (August, 1991), pp. 3.1 -3.16.

24 Wolfson, pp. 3.6 - 3.7.

25 Fellegi, p. 4.17.

26 Murphy and Wolfson, p. ii.

27 Murphy and Wolfson, p. 19.

28 Ellen Gee and Susan McDaniel, "Pension Politics and Challenges: Retirement Policy Implications," *Canadian Public Policy*, 17, 4 (1991), p. 458.

29 Ibid. p. 458.

30 Organisation for Economic Cooperation and Development, "Labour Market Participation and Retirement of Older Workers," *Employment Outlook*, July 1992 (Paris: OECD, 1992), p. 213.

CHAPTER SEVEN

1 David Foot and Kevin Gibson, "Population Aging in the Canadian Labour Force: Changes and Challenges," *Journal of Canadian Studies*, 28, 1 (Spring, 1993), p. 61.

2 Ibid.

3 Organization for Economic Cooperation and Development, "Labour Market Participation and Retirement of Older Workers," *Employment Outlook*, July 1992 (Paris: OECD, 1992), p. 196.

4 Chief Actuary, Office of the Superintendent of Financial Institutions, Ottawa. Quoted in Andrew Coyne, "The burden of our pensions," *Globe and Mail*, Monday, August 15, 1994, p. A8.

5 Nancy Zukewich Ghalam, "Women in the Workplace," *Canadian Social Trends*, 28 (Spring 1993), pp. 4-5.

6 Cameron W. Stout, "A degree of change," *Perspectives on Labour and Income*, 4, 4 (Winter 1992), p. 15.

7 Ghalam, p. 5.

8 Economic Council of Canada, *Good Jobs, Bad Jobs: Employment in the Service Economy* (Ottawa: The Economic Council of Canada, 1990).

9 Also see: G. Picot, J. Myles and T. Wannell, "Good Jobs/Bad Jobs and the Declining Middle: 1967-1986." Statistics Canada, Analytical Studies Branch, Paper No. 28, 1990; R. Morissette, J. Myles, G. Picot, "What is Happening to Earnings Inequality in Canada." Statistics Canada, Analytical Studies Branch, Paper No. 60, 1993.

BIBLIOGRAPHY

Achdut, Lea and Yossi Tamir. "Retirement and Well-being Among the Elderly." *Poverty, Inequality and Income Distribution in Comparative Perspective, The Luxembourg Income Study.* Ed. Timothy Smeeding, et al. Washington, D.C.: The Urban Institute Press, 1990, 105-125.

Akyeampong, Ernest. "Job Loss and Labour Market Adjustment." *The Labour Force.* Ottawa: Minister of Supply and Services, Cat. 71-001, (March, 1987), 107-120.

Akyeampong, Ernest. "Older Workers in the Canadian Labour Market." *The Labour Force.* Ottawa: Minister of Supply and Services, Cat. 71-001, (November, 1987), 85-120.

Akyeampong, Ernest. "Flexitime work arrangements." *Perspectives on Labour and Income.* Vol. 5, No. 3 (Autumn, 1993), 17-22.

Bazzoli, Gloria. "The early retirement decision, New empirical evidence on the influence of health." *Journal of Human Resources.* Vol. 20 No. 2 (Spring, 1985), 97-101.

Boaz, Rachel Floersheim. "Early Withdrawal from the Labor Force, A Response Only to Pension Pull or Also to Labor Market Push." *Research on Aging.* Vol. 9, No 4 (1988), 530-547.

Bridges to Retirement, Older Workers in a Changing Labor Market. Ed. Peter Doeringer. Ithaca, N.Y.: ILR Press, Cornell University, 1990.

Bryden, W. Kenneth. *Old Age Pensions and Policy Making in Canada.* Ph.D. Thesis, University of Toronto, 1970.

Chirikos, Thomas and Gilbert Nestel. "Occupational Differences in the Ability of Men to Delay Retirement." *The Journal of Human Resources.* Vol. 26, No. 1 (1991), 1-27.

Clement, Wallace and John Myles. *Relations of Ruling, Class and Gender in Postindustrial Societies.* Montreal: McGill-Queen's University Press, 1994.

Denton, Frank and Sylvia Ostry. *Working-Life Tables for Canadian Males.* Ottawa: Dominion Bureau of Statistics, 1969.

Ekerdt, David, Barbara Vinich and Raymond Bosse. "Orderly Endings, Do Men Know When They Will Retire?" *Journal of Gerontology.* 44, 1 (1989), S28-S35.

Esping-Andersen, Gosta and Harald Sonnberger. "The Demographic of Age in Labor-Market Management." *States, Labor Markets, and the Future of Old-Age Policy.* Ed. John Myles and Jill Quadagno. Philadelphia: University Press, 1991, 227-249.

Family Security in Insecure Times. The National Forum on Family Security. Ottawa: Canadian Council on Social Development, 1993.

Fellegi, Ivan. "Can We Afford an Aging Society." *Canadian Economic Observer.* (October, 1988), 4.1 - 4.34.

Fields, Gary S. and Olivia S. Mitchell. *Retirement, Pensions, and Social Security.* Cambridge: The MIT Press, 1984.

Fillembaum, Gerda, Linda George and Erdman Palmore. "Determinants and Consequences of Retirement Among Men of Different Races and Economic Levels." *Journal of Gerontology.* Vol. 40, No. 1 (1985), 85-94.

Foot, David and Kevin Gibson. "Population Aging in the Canadian Labour Force, Changes and Challenges." *Journal of Canadian Studies.* Vol. 28, No. 1 (Spring, 1993), 59-74.

Foster, Chris. *Towards a National Retirement Incomes Policy.* Social Security Review, Australia, Issues Paper No. 6, 1988.

Frenken, Hubert. "Women and RRSPs." *Perspectives on Labour and Income.* Vol. 3, No. 4 (Winter, 1991), 8-13.

Frenken, Hubert. "Marriage, money and retirement." *Perspectives on Labour and Income.* Vol. 3, No. 4 (Winter 1991), 31-34.

Frenken, Hubert and Karen Maser. "Employer-sponsored pension plans—who is covered?" *Perspectives on Labour and Income.* Vol. 4, No. 4 (Winter 1992), 27-34.

Fuchs, Victor. "Self-Employment and Labor Force Participation of Older Males." *Journal of Human Resources.* Vol. 17, No. 3 (1982), 339-358.

Galarneau, Diane. "Women approaching retirement." *Perspectives on Labour and Income.* Vol. 3, No. 3 (Autumn, 1991), 28-39.

Gee, Ellen and Susan McDaniel. "Pension Politics and Challenges, Retirement Policy Implications." *Canadian Public Policy.* Vol. 17, No. 4 (1991), 456-472.

George, Linda, Gerda Fillenbaum and Erdman Palmore. "Sex Differences in the Antecedents and Consequences of Retirement." *Journal of Gerontology.* Vol. 39, No. 3 (1984), 364-371.

Graebner, William. *A History of Retirement, The Meaning and Function of An American Institution, 1885-1978.* New Haven: Yale University Press, 1980.

Guillemard, Anne-Marie. "International Perspectives on Early Withdrawal from the Labour Force." *States, Labor Markets, and the Future of Old-Age Policy.* Ed. John Myles and Jill Quadagno. Philadelphia: University Press, (1991), pp. 209-226.

Guillemard, Anne-Marie and Herman van Gunsteren. "Pathways and their prospects, A comparative interpretation of the meaning of early retirement." *Time for Retirement: Comparative Studies of Early Exit from the Labour Force.* Ed. Martin Kohli et al. Cambridge: Cambridge University Press, 1991, 382-387.

Gunderson, Morley and James Pesando. "The Case for Allowing Mandatory Retirement." *Canadian Public Policy.* Vol 14, No. 1 (1988), 32-39.

Hayward, M., W. Grady, M. Hardy and D. Sommers. "Occupational Influences on Retirement, Disability, and Death." *Demography.* Vol. 26, No. 3 (1989), 393-409.

Hayward, Mark and William Grady. "Work and Retirement Among a Cohort of Older Men in the United States, 1966-1983." *Demography.* Vol. 27, No. 3 (1990), 337-356.

Henretta, John, Christopher Chan, and Angela O'Rand. "Retirement Reason Versus Retirement Process: Examining the Reasons for Retirement Typology." *Journal of Gerontology.* Vol. 47, No. 1 (1992), S1-S7.

Industrial Relations Plans in Canada. Industrial Relations Section, School of Commerce and Administration, Queen's University. Kingston: Queen's University, 1938.

Jackson, Michael. "Early retirement: recent trends and implications." *Industrial Relations Journal*. Vol. 15, No. 3 (Autumn 1984), 21-28.

Kohli, Martin and Martin Rein. "The changing balance of work and retirement." *Time for Retirement: Comparative Studies of Early Exit from the Labour Force*. Ed. Martin Kohli et al. Cambridge: Cambridge University Press, 1991, 1-35.

Krahn, Harvey. "Non-standard work arrangements." *Perspectives on Labour and Income*. Vol.3, No. 4 (Winter, 1991), 35-45.

Krashinsky, Michael. "The Case for Eliminating Mandatory Retirement, Why Economics and Human Rights Need Not Conflict." *Canadian Public Policy*. Vol. 14, No. 1 (1988), 40-51.

Laczko, Frank. "Early Retirement in a Period of High Unemployment." *Journal of Social Policy*. Vol. 17, No. 3 (1988), 313-333.

Laczko, Frank. "Between Work and Retirement, Becoming 'Old' in the 1980s." *Becoming and Being Old, Sociological Approaches to Later Life*. Ed. Bill Bytheway et al. London: Sage Publications, 1989, 24-40.

Laczko, Frank and Chris Phillipson. *Changing Work and Retirement, Social Policy and the Older Worker*. Philadelphia: Open University Press, 1991.

Leon, Joel. "The Effects of Labor Market Segmentation on Economic Resources in Retirement." *Social Science Research*. Vol. 14, (1985), 351-373.

Marshall, Victor and Barry McPherson. "Aging, Canadian Perspectives." *Journal of Canadian Studies*. Vol. 28, No. 1 (Spring, 1993), 3-13.

McDaniel, Susan. "Demographic Aging as a Guiding Paradigm in Canada's Welfare State." *Canadian Public Policy*. Vol. 13, No. 3 (September 1987), 330-336.

McDonald, Lynn and Mervin Chen. "The Youth Freeze and the Retirement Bulge, Older Workers and the Impending Labour Shortage." *Journal of Canadian Studies*. Vol. 28, No. 1 (Spring, 1993), 75-101.

Mitchell, Olivia, Phillip Levine and Silvana Pozzebon. "Retirement Differences by Industry and Occupation." *The Gerontologist*. Vol. 28, No. 4 (1988), 545-551.

Moore, Maureen. "Dual-Earner Families, The New Norm." *Canadian Social Trends*. No. 12 (Spring, 1989), 24-26.

Murphy, Brian and Michael Wolfson. "When the Baby Boom Grows Old: Impacts on Canada's Public Sector." Statistics Canada, Analytical Studies Branch, Paper No. 38, 1991.

Myers, Robert. "Why Do People Retire from Work Early." *Social Security Bulletin*. Vol. 45, (1982), 10-14.

Myles, John. *Old Age in the Welfare State, The Political Economy of Public Pensions*. Revised Edition. Kansas: University Press of Kansas, 1989.

Myles, John and Les Teichroew, "The Politics of Dualism, Pension Policy in Canada." *States, Labor Markets, and the Future of Old-Age Policy*. Ed. John Myles and Jill Quadagno. Philadelphia: Temple University Press, 1991, 84-104.

National Council of Welfare. *A Pension Primer*. Ottawa: Minister of Supply and Services Canada, Cat.H68-23/1989, 1989.

National Council of Welfare. *Pension Reform*. Ottawa: Minister of Supply and Services Canada, Cat.H68-24/1990, 1990.

Organisation for Economic Co-operation and Development. "Labour Market Participation and Retirement of Older Workers." *Employment Outlook, July 1992.* Paris: OECD, July, 1992, 195-237.

Organisation for Economic Co-operation and Development. "The Transition from Work to Retirement." *New Orientations for Social Policy.* Social Policy Studies No. 12. Paris: OECD, 1994, 27-36.

Osberg, Lars. "Is It Retirement or Unemployment? The Constrained Labour Supply of Older Canadians." Statistics Canada, October, 1988.

Parnes, Herbert. "The Retirement Decision." *The Older Worker.* Madison: Industrial Relations Research Association, 1988, 115-150.

Phillipson, Chris. *Capitalism and the Construction of Old Age.* London: The MacMillan Press Ltd. 1982.

Schellenberg, Grant. "Benefits for part-time workers." *Perception.* Vol. 18, No. 1 (1994), 14-16.

Schuller, Tom. "Work-Ending, Employment and Ambiguity in Later Life." *Becoming and Being Old, Sociological Approaches to Later Life.* Ed. Bill Bytheway et al. London: Sage Publications, 1989, pp. 41-54.

Seniors Secretariat. *Ageing and Independence, Overview of a National Survey.* Ottawa: Minister of Supply and Services Canada, 1993. Cat. H88-3/13-1993.

Siroonian, Jason. "A note on the recession and early retirement." *Perspectives on Labour and Income.* Vol. 5, No. 4 (Winter 1993), 9-11.

Tindale, Joseph. *Older Workers in an Aging Work Force.* Ottawa: National Advisory Council on Aging, Cat. H71-2/1-10-1991E, 1991.

Vanier Institute of the Family, *Profiling Canada's Families.* Ottawa: Vanier Institute of the Family, 1994.

Wolfson, Michael. "International Perspectives on the Economics of Aging." *Canadian Economic Observer.* (August, 1991), 3.1 -3.16.